VOLUME 2

EXPERIENCES OF PUNISHMENT, ABUSE AND JUSTICE BY WOMEN AND FAMILIES

Edited by
Natalie Booth, Isla Masson and Lucy Baldwin

With a foreword by Anita Dockley

P

First published in Great Britain in 2023 by

Policy Press, an imprint of
Bristol University Press
University of Bristol
1–9 Old Park Hill
Bristol
BS2 8BB
UK
t: +44 (0)117 374 6645
e: bup-info@bristol.ac.uk

Details of international sales and distribution partners are available at policy.bristoluniversitypress.co.uk

British Library Cataloguing in Publication Data
A catalogue record for this book is available from the British Library

ISBN 978-1-4473-6390-3 hardcover
ISBN 978-1-4473-6391-0 paperback
ISBN 978-1-4473-6392-7 ePub
ISBN 978-1-4473-6393-4 ePdf

Cover design: Hayes Design and Advertising
Front cover image: Ed Barrett

Contents

Notes on contributors

Laura Abbott is Senior Lecturer in Midwifery at the University of Hertfordshire, a senior fellow of the Higher Education Academy and a fellow of the Royal College of Midwives. Laura's doctorate examined the experiences of pregnant women in prison: *The Incarcerated Pregnancy: An Ethnographic Study of Perinatal Women in English Prisons*. Laura volunteers with the charity Birth Companions and co-authored their *Birth Charter* (Birth Companions, 2016). She has also contributed to the review of operational policy for prison staff managing and caring for all women experiencing pregnancy, Mother and Baby Units (MBUs) and maternal separation in prison. In September 2020 Laura was awarded the Mildred Blaxter Post-Doctoral Fellowship from the Foundation for the Sociology of Health and Illness to continue with her research into the experiences of imprisoned perinatal women.

Gemma Ahearne is Lecturer in Criminology at the School of Law and Social Justice, University of Liverpool, UK. Gemma has 20 years' experience of the sex industry and her research and teaching focuses on vulnerability, stigma and moralising discourses. She is committed to scholarship on pedagogy, sex work, women in prison and the criminal justice system (CJS), and violence against women.

Lucy Baldwin is Associate Professor at Durham University. Lucy has worked in criminal and social justice for over 30 years, also being a qualified social worker and probation officer. Her research and academic publications focus predominantly on the impact of imprisonment on mothers and their children. Lucy's work informed the Female Offender Strategy, the Farmer Review and the Joint Human Rights Inquiry into Maternal Imprisonment and the Rights of the Child. She also co-convenes the Women, Family, Crime and Justice (WFCJ) research network.

Rebecca Barnes is Senior Research Adviser in Qualitative and Social Research Methods at the NIHR Research Design Service East Midlands, based at the University of Leicester. She was also recently appointed as senior lecturer in Social Research Methods in the School of Pharmacy at the University of Lincoln. In this new fractional role, she co-leads an NIHR-funded project which focuses on providing access to support for domestic abuse and suicidal thoughts via community pharmacies. Rebecca has been researching domestic abuse for 20 years, with particular expertise in LGBT+ people's domestic abuse victimisation, perpetration and help seeking. She has also researched church responses to domestic abuse. She published *Queering*

Narratives of Domestic Violence and Abuse (Palgrave Macmillan) with Catherine Donovan in 2020.

Somia R. Bibi is a sociologist and researcher who joined Himaya Haven CIC as a volunteer and is now their Family Engagement and Outreach Worker. She is presently writing up her University of Warwick Economic and Social Research Council (ESRC)-funded thesis, which explores the experiences of racialised beauty of British South Asian women, with a nuanced exploration of skin colour and shadeism. She has worked for over six years in higher education, both lecturing and researching. Working within the community alongside undertaking research is a long-term passion.

Natalie Booth is Senior Lecturer in Criminology at Bath Spa University. Her research and publications contribute to our understanding about the maintenance of relationships and family contact during imprisonment, the experience of mothers and women in prison, remand and developments in penal policy relating to women and families in England and Wales. She also co-convenes the WFCJ research network.

Anita Dockley is the Howard League for Penal Reform's research director. She is responsible for developing the charity's research capacity, forging links with academics and universities, funders and partner organisations. Her own research interests include suicide and self-harm in prisons, women in prison and order and control in the prison environment. Anita is the managing editor of the *Howard Journal of Crime and Justice*. She is a member of the ESRC Grant Assessment Panel and has been a Research Excellence Framework (REF) panel member in 2021 and 2014. She is an honorary visiting fellow in the School of History, Politics and International Relations at the University of Leicester and a research associate at Liverpool John Moores University.

Catherine Donovan is Professor of Sociology in the Department of Sociology at Durham University, UK. Catherine has spent nearly 30 years researching the intimate and family lives of lesbians, gay men and, more recently, bisexual and trans people. With Marianne Hester, she conducted the first research project comparing love and violence in the relationships of heterosexual and same-sex relationships. More recently, with Rebecca Barnes, she has conducted research on the use of violence and abusive behaviours by LGB and/or T+ people. Currently, she is also conducting research on hate relationships, home takeovers and sexual violence/ harassment in universities.

Razia Tariq Hadait is CEO/Founding Director of Himaya Haven CIC and has been recognised with an MBE on the Queen's birthday honours list 2022 for her services to the Birmingham community. She has been a community activist for 24 years, championing the needs of disadvantaged groups from diverse, ethnic minority communities living in the most deprived areas of Birmingham. Razia has worked across the third sector in multiple roles, thus gaining frontline expertise in community issues and how to support those in need. Throughout the years she has also been raising awareness of taboo issues within local communities such as forced marriage, female genital mutilation, domestic violence, honour-based violence, child sexual exploitation and sexual abuse within the family environment. Razia continues to advocate for and support those who have been disenfranchised, isolated and forgotten, like families and individuals who have a loved one in custody or prison.

Zobia Hadait is a company director/secretary of Himaya Haven CIC alongside the website and social media manager. She has been a part of Himaya Haven since its inception. Presently, she is the project coordinator and lead researcher for Himaya Haven's Heritage Art project, funded by the Heritage Lottery. This project involves HMP Swinfen Hall prisoners who are using different art mediums to share the history of the prison. Zobia has a first-class degree in Psychology and a master's degree in Cyberpsychology. Her dissertations included looking at boredom proneness and Instagram usage and the effect of binge watching TV streaming platforms on mental health and wellbeing.

Jenny Mackay is Senior Lecturer in Forensic Psychology at Nottingham Trent University. She is a chartered psychologist, and has spent many years working in practitioner-facing roles with vulnerable clients in both forensic and non-forensic settings. Her research focuses on understanding and intervening with perpetration of intimate partner violence.

Isla Masson is a criminologist and Researcher at the Open University. Her research interests include women in the CJS, motherhood, incarceration, remand, care leavers and restorative justice. Her book *Incarcerating Motherhood* (Routledge, 2019) was based on her doctoral research, which explored the longevity of short terms of incarceration on mothers. She is a trustee at the Boaz Project, which is a therapeutic work environment for adults with learning disabilities, and previously volunteered with the Independent Monitoring Board. She also co-convenes the WFCJ research network.

Jo Smith is Senior Lecturer in Law at the University of Brighton. She completed her PhD at the University of Surrey, looking at how feminist women experience, explain and respond to online gendered hate. She has subsequently published several book chapters exploring this topic, has recently co-edited the book *Misogyny as Hate Crime* (Routledge, 2021) and is currently co-authoring a book looking at hate crime perpetration. Her research interests include hate crime, online abuse, gender-based violence and feminist research methods. She also works with Rights of Women as a legal adviser.

Acknowledgements

To our loved ones, including the newest arrivals: know that you are always at the centre of everything that we do and that we are so very grateful to have you in our lives. We are also extremely appreciative of the time and energy that has been poured into this collection by our contributors during what have been some of the most difficult times. Likewise, without their service users/clients and supporters, the contributors' work would not be able to shed light on the many experiences and challenges continuing to face women and families in our communities. Our deepest thanks go to you all.

Natalie, Isla and Lucy

Foreword: time to shift the focus and reduce the use of the penal system for women

Anita Dockley

More than 30 years ago I started working in penal reform. For the entirety of this time women have represented around 5 per cent of the prison population of England and Wales (House of Commons Library, 2021). Yet this, as all commentators on the criminal justice system (CJS) know, is just the tip of the iceberg, with thousands of other women directly affected by the penal system through community sentences or supporting other family members. Despite the best efforts of academic research, practitioner concerns, parliamentary scrutiny and campaigners like the Howard League for Penal Reform, this statistic seems intractable. But this should not be so.

In recent times there has been much political interest in women in the CJS. The Female Offender Strategy (FOS) (Ministry of Justice [MoJ], 2018) aimed to shift the focus away from the penal system through earlier intervention and community support, and community sentences rather than prison sentences (especially short ones). It also sought to create better conditions for women in custody, for example, by improving and maintaining family ties, reducing self-harm and providing better support on release. Yet several years on there seems to be little progress. The recent National Audit Office report (2022) found it hard to establish what progress had been made. In part, this was due to the lack of clarity in the initial plan – for instance, actions mixed into narrative, a lack of public-facing information and a lack of inter-governmental department working.

Perplexingly, the Prisons Strategy White Paper (MoJ, 2021) seemed to take the opposite tack to the FOS (MoJ, 2018) by focusing on investing in prisons and expanding their capacity. For women this included the announcement of 500 more prison places. In the foreword to the White Paper, the then Justice Secretary Dominic Raab sought views on 'how the proposals can bring down stubbornly high rates of reoffending, cut crime and protect the public from harm'. Yet the plans don't stack up: they do not allow for the development of regimes with time out of cell to ensure there are opportunities to socialise, receive visits from their loved ones and take part in meaningful work and/or education – all factors which are known to support effective reintegration into communities and increase the potential of women living a crime-free life following prison. The joint Chief Inspectors' report into the impact of COVID-19 on the CJS was particularly critical of the prison system, with them indicating that 'If prisoners are successfully to rejoin the wider community when they are released, they need to be educated and trained for work, allowed to maintain contact with their families and given the support they need to address their offending behaviour by an effective and well-trained staff team' (Criminal Justice Joint Inspection, 2022, p 4).

Numerous reports, not least the Corston Report back in 2007, conclude that prison is rarely a necessary, appropriate or proportionate response to women who offend. In the wake of her report, Baroness Corston established the All-Party Parliamentary Group (APPG) on women in the penal system, which receives administrative and research support from the Howard League for Penal Reform. It works to increase knowledge and awareness of issues around women in the penal system as well as push for full implementation of the recommendations of her report. The APPG has focused on many aspects of the penal system as it impacts on women from arrests (Howard League for Penal Reform, 2021) to remand (Howard League for Penal Reform, 2020), and it is currently looking at women's health and wellbeing when they are sent to prison (Howard League for Penal Reform, 2022). It contends that women are going into prison in poor health and that the unhealthy prison environment exacerbates this. Evidence includes poor living conditions, retraumatisation of women through the prison practice of strip search and the use of mechanical restraints and ultimately a prison system that was designed around the needs of men in prison.

Current thinking about the penal system is skewed. Instead of a scarce resource with prison and punishment as a last resort, the last 30 years has seen an explosion of criminal justice-orientated legislation: some 78 law and order Acts with a further ten proposed in the 2022 Queen's speech. By comparison, in the preceding 20 years there had been considerably fewer pieces of criminal justice-orientated legislation, with 23 law and order Acts. What does this say about our society? More fearful and quicker to punish? It appears that the learning about the people who are subjected to the CJS generally, but more particularly regarding women, is not cutting through. Research, much like the findings in this book, have repeatedly focused on women's complex and multiple needs including mental health concerns, abusive (past) relationships, homelessness, addictions and caring responsibilities. So, I believe as a society there is a failure to invest in the policy areas which could really drive a shift away from an overuse of an ineffective penal system. There needs to be a rethinking and a reorientating of social and health policies to more effectively enable women (people) to succeed. Support, thinking and resources that could make a real difference to outcomes for women who currently enter the penal system. In short, the answers and practice we need to be thinking about lie outside the CJS: the MoJ and the Home Office cannot resolve the issues.

As such, this this book on the experiences of punishment, abuse and justice by women and families is an incredibly timely collection. It is seeking to move the debate on, and I hope prompt support for the overdue shift of focus away from the penal system but also to invest more effectively in the women who are subject to it. The voices it amplifies and the topics it covers should make everyone stop and think about the realities of the penal system for women in England and Wales. And hopefully think, it *is* time to shift the focus.

References

Criminal Justice Joint Inspection (2022) The impact of the COVID-19 pandemic on the criminal justice system – a progress report, [online] 17 May. Available from: www.justiceinspectorates.gov.uk/cjji/wp-content/uploads/sites/2/2022/05/CJ-Covid-19-recovery-progress-report-web-2022.pdf [Accessed: 19 May 2022].

Howard League for Penal Reform (2020) Reset: rethinking remand for women, Howard League for Penal Reform, [online]. Available from: https://howardleague.org/wp-content/uploads/2020/07/Rethinking-remand-for-women.pdf [Accessed: 19 May 2022].

Howard League for Penal Reform (2021) Arresting the entry of women into the criminal justice system: briefing three, [online]. Available from: https://howardleague.org/wp-content/uploads/2021/05/APPG-on-Women-in-the-Penal-System-briefing-3-FINAL.pdf [Accessed: 19 May 2022].

Howard League for Penal Reform (2022) Inquiry into women's health and well-being in prisons: briefing one, [online]. Available from: https://howardleague.org/wp-content/uploads/2021/08/clinks-APPG-women-health-and-wellbeing-in-prison-final-draft-190521.pdf [Accessed: 19 May 2022].

Ministry of Justice (MoJ) (2018) *Female Offender Strategy*, London: Ministry of Justice, [online] June. Available from: https://assets.publishing.service.gov.uk/government/uploads/system/uploads/attachment_data/file/719819/female-offender-strategy.pdf [Accessed: 19 May 2022].

MoJ (2021) *Prisons Strategy White Paper*, London: Ministry of Justice, [online], December. Available from: https://assets.publishing.service.gov.uk/government/uploads/system/uploads/attachment_data/file/1038765/prisons-strategy-white-paper.pdf [Accessed: 19 May 2022].

National Audit Office (2022) Improving outcomes for women in the criminal justice system, [online] 19 January. Available from: www.nao.org.uk/reports/improving-outcomes-for-women-in-the-criminal-justice-system/ [Accessed: 19 May 2022].

Sturge, G. (2021) UK prison population statistics, House of Commons Library, [online] 29 October. Available from: https://researchbriefings.files.parliament.uk/documents/SN04334/SN04334.pdf [Accessed: 19 May 2022].

Keeping the conversation going: the Women, Family, Crime and Justice network

Natalie Booth, Lucy Baldwin and Isla Masson

Introduction

We are delighted to present this second volume of evidence and ideas emerging from the Women, Family, Crime and Justice (WFCJ) network. The WFCJ network, and its publications, are focused on drawing attention to current, real-life issues relating to the experiences, perceptions and social and criminal justice environments for women and families. Central to this aim is the sharing of knowledge in an attempt to bring about positive change and further reflection on the social injustices that trouble our communities. Specifically, this collection shines a light on experiences of punishment, abuse and justice as experienced by women and families in several different, but overlapping, areas of contemporary society.

We make no secret of the fact that we, the editors, are deeply concerned with the lack of meaningful change for women and families to date. While the increased attention and focus directed towards the challenging social and criminal justice issues facing women and families in England and Wales is something to celebrate, we remain frustrated that the growing evidence base and catalogue of campaigns are leading to limited implementation at policy level. Previously, we commented: 'it is disheartening to say that much-needed change has been slow to [be] actualised' (Masson, Booth and Baldwin, 2021, p 1). This view was shaped from our critical review of the Female Offender Strategy (FOS) (Ministry of Justice [MoJ], 2018) in which we predicted that the string of 'promises' would be ineffectual owing to the lack of meaningful strategies and policies presented (Booth, Masson and Baldwin, 2018). Since then, and as highlighted by Anita Dockley in the foreword to this collection, the situation seems to have deteriorated. To recap, we have seen some worrying U-turns including the MoJ announcement in January 2021 that an additional 500 prison places would be created for women as a result of increased policing (MoJ, 2021). Although the stated intention is to make the new spaces 'better' spaces – with some intended to facilitate child stays – we believe the emphasis and allocated funds should lie with increased community provision. This would allow more women/mothers to be diverted away from custody and prevent the separation of mothers from their children by imprisonment at all. Thus, we believe that to build these 'new' spaces, without closing down the equivalent number of 'old' spaces, is exceptionally punitive and misunderstood. As Baldwin (2021) has stated elsewhere, the closure of spaces in the closed prison estate would be especially preferable given how these environments are additionally punitive for mothers. During the last couple of years two extremely heartbreaking events in the UK resulting in the deaths of two babies born to imprisoned women have occurred. The findings from the inquiry into two baby deaths, one in HMP Bronzefield (Prison and Probation Ombudsman, 2021) and one in HMP Styal (Prison and Probation Ombudsman, 2022) are exceptionally disturbing and seriously bring into question current practices. What is more, the proposed changes to the female prison estate completely disregard long-standing evidence around the effectiveness of prison for women and are contrary to the government's own stated intentions in the FOS.

Taken together, it is increasingly clear that the many concerns and issues we anticipated and highlighted with the 'promises' of the FOS have indeed resulted in this policy initiative seriously failing. Therefore, the important contributions enclosed in this edited collection, alongside the turbulent times we are all living through, reinforce our belief that continued discussion and critical reflection are needed more than ever. Furthermore, the impact of the COVID-19 pandemic on the criminal justice system (CJS) has led to overly punitive carceral experiences for reasons of public health (Edgar et al, 2021). This has occurred from criminal justice responses such as the 23-hour lock-up of prisoners and the suspension of visits between prisoners and their loved ones (including mother–child contact). Such changes have contributed to the already traumatic experience that is imprisonment, while the cessation of visits was contrary to the advice of the Joint Committee on Human Rights (2020). Babies born to mothers in prison during COVID-19 were not even permitted to meet their fathers, meaning some babies had their first birthdays in prison without ever having met fathers and loved ones. COVID-19 restrictions have exacerbated court delays for those on remand and awaiting trial, adding further trauma to the accused, and their loved ones in the community (Booth and Masson, 2021). The ripple effects of these prolonged periods of separation will impact on families for many years to come.

In the community COVID-19 lockdowns led to a surge in poor mental health, higher levels of substance misuse and increased use of violence against women and other vulnerable individuals (Havard, 2021). Critically, the lockdowns have highlighted the gaps between the 'haves' and the 'have nots' by emphasising social disadvantage. For instance, food poverty and the issues surrounding free school meals (Food Foundation, 2020), as well as access to digital devices and platforms to enable online/remote working and learning, have led to further social exclusion of some. We have also seen harrowing reports of attacks against women, as was highly publicised in the case of Sarah Everard (Casciani, 2021), and protests following the unlawful killing of George Floyd (Konadu and Gyamfi, 2021), which have highlighted unacceptable, systemic inequalities in our society. While this list is by no means exhaustive, we are confident that as more evidence emerges, we will see the widening of social divisions that already exist, as well as the specific damage this has brought to women and families. Likewise, reflecting on the social context at the time of writing provides an important reminder of the challenging circumstances that we have *all* been trying to negotiate (albeit to varying degrees) recently. This includes the researchers and practitioners have who have taken the time and energy to contribute to this collection.

Introducing the second volume/current collection

The three editors of this book have co-convened the network since its birth in 2018, having come together through our shared research and social justice interests in women and families affected by the CJS (see Masson, Baldwin and Booth, 2021 for more information). The intention of the WFCJ network was to enable the sharing of important conversations and reflections on the experiences, practices, policies and research findings developing in this broad and interdisciplinary field. The WFCJ research network sits at an intersection that is purposefully broad to capture the imagination and engagement of frontline practitioners, policy makers, service users, students and researchers in interrelated fields, but all with a shared interest in bringing about positive change to tackle the inequalities and the challenges facing women and families. This is predominantly achieved through our seminar series, mailing list and presence on Twitter. As the network has a strong following, we wanted to seize the opportunity to draw on this interest and momentum to produce a second book.

We are proud that this second volume compliments the first book while being distinct in its focus and remit. It sheds light on a different set of issues facing women and families, and very much warranting our attention. This shift in focus is an outcome of our joint reflection on the voices that were elevated in the first volume, and the opportunity to 'be more representative' (Baldwin, Masson and Booth, 2021, p 224). In acknowledging how we are all products of our histories, we asked uncomfortable questions of ourselves – and of our network – to identify who/what had been privileged and who/what was absent. These reflections instigated a purposeful redirection which means that this second volume includes issues and challenges that shape the lives and experiences of a diverse range of women and families. For instance, this includes LGB and/or T+ experiences of domestic abuse support services, Black, Asian and Minority Ethnic (BAME) families' experiences of imprisonment and online misogyny, among others. We think that each chapter provides a fascinating insight into issues facing women and families, with new contributors writing about their research, professional roles, community-based organisations and lived experiences.

Drawing on their findings, we invited contributors to make recommendations for change and to indicate where we might seek to drive new policies and practices in the future for the betterment of the populations with which they engage. Tangible and practical recommendations are therefore a common feature of the chapters, with bottom-up, service user-informed change being proposed. Moreover, the authors have produced current and relevant conversations for the reader to engage with and, as part of this, have included reflection points, or questions, at the end of their contributions. These reflection points seek to encourage the reader to reflect on their learning from the chapter, to question their assumptions and to consider if/how changes might be brought to their own thinking and working environment to challenge the status quo. Finally, it is important to highlight that the book has been divided thematically into two parts. Organising the book in this way seeks to guide the reader, though there are overarching issues and findings throughout which have been highlighted when appropriate.

Chapter overview

The first theme, *Punishing women in the criminal justice system*, includes three chapters that seek to illuminate the gendered pains of prison and community sanctions for women who have been subjected to ineffectual policy and practice. In Chapter 2 Laura Abbott, a midwifery academic and researcher, presents original empirical findings from a pilot study that sought to illuminate the experiences of 'supporters' working in women's prisons with expectant mothers. The 'supporters' interviewed comprised of women with experience of providing pregnancy and birth support in English prisons, and their reflections on how support provisions and services were adversely affected by the COVID-19 pandemic. Abbott indicates how prison was already found to be an unhealthy and inappropriate place for pregnant women before the COVID-19 virus, but that the impact of changes during the pandemic severely harmed this particularly vulnerable population. By combining the new findings with existing evidence regarding pregnancy in prison, this chapter is an essential read for those interested in the punitive ways in which the CJS inexplicably punishes incarcerated pregnant women.

Taking a different approach in Chapter 3, Gemma Ahearne, an academic with lived experience of the CJS, writes auto/biographical reflections from working in one women's centre in the north of England, recounting (re) traumatising practices that she felt undermined the ethos of empowering women. Ahearne contends that the use of women's centres as an alternative to custody is generally celebrated, but that failing to question policies and practices that may occur in some centres can significantly harm the very women who are meant to be supported. This chapter questions whether women's centres are there to 'empower or punish', and the revelations shared in Ahearne's reflections indicate the potential outcomes that can occur from a paradox generated in this gendered space. While not necessarily reflective of all women's centres, importantly, this chapter invites the reader to think critically about the role of women's centres and the way in which these are conceptualised and operationalised within the current neoliberal climate in England.

Chapter 4 rounds off the first theme by focusing on the diverse and varied ways that the CJS punishes female loved ones with an incarcerated relative in England. The authors, Zobia Hadait, Somia Bibi and Razia Tariq Hadait, are practitioners working at Himaya Haven CIC, a community-based organisation based in Birmingham, England, supporting prisoners and their families. While their services are accessible to all, Himaya Haven clientele tend to self-identify as BAME women, and so the chapter draws attention to the cultural and gendered issues that their clients face in the event of arrest and imprisonment of a loved one. The authors include voices of their service users alongside their practitioner reflections to articulate the distressing circumstances that are a reality for the BAME women, children and young people that they support. Outlining provisions accessible to Himaya Haven clients, and the importance of joined-up inter-agency work, the authors argue that little meaningful change can be achieved while prisoners' families remain 'silent victims' in wider society.

The second theme of the collection, *Violence, abuse and justice*, is made up of three chapters that each draw attention to violent and abusive behaviours in both intimate relationships and online spaces, and the responses (or shortcomings) of criminal justice agencies. In Chapter 5 academic researchers Rebecca Barnes and Catherine Donovan present findings from their study exploring LGB and/or T+ people's use of abusive behaviours. Drawing on data from focus groups with practitioners from 'relationship services', this chapter highlights the woeful lack of attention, services and consistent support available to LGB and/or T+ people in abusive intimate relationships. These findings stand in stark contrast to the increased awareness and support for heterosexual and cisgender women in similar circumstances in recent years. Articulating the acute and harmful impact of this unmet need, the authors propose practical recommendations to help rebalance the unacceptable inequalities observed, making it an important read for many working in related fields, including practitioners, policy makers and voluntary sector organisations.

Also presenting new research findings on abusive intimate partner relationships, academic researcher Jenny Mackay explores abuse perpetrated by imprisoned women in Chapter 6. The findings present new insights into the pathways, functions and offence processes involved in intimate partner violence and abuse (IPVA) perpetrated by the women. Interestingly, the chapter reveals how this behaviour should be understood in the context of the women's lives, indicating how complex trauma and chaotic living situations were perpetuating factors, as well as motivations to assume some control and/or prevent further harm being inflicted on them. From the nuanced insights provided, recommendations point towards the need for individualised, gendered, trauma-informed practices so that justice responses can adequately support women and prevent further harm.

Chapter 7 also draws attention to women's experiences of abusive practices through qualitative research. Academic researcher Jo Smith presents new empirical findings on online misogyny. This research highlights the negative experiences of formal routes to justice for women who have been victimised as there is scepticism about the extent to which their abuse will be effectively managed. Instead, what is fascinating about the findings are the alternative strategies to online gendered abuse which involve action – sometimes collective resistance – by women which then resulted in feelings of empowerment and support. While not always risk-free, these alternative strategies indicate how existing routes to justice fail women, but that the coming together of women in online spaces is an example of contemporary feminist activism.

Concluding thoughts

We are delighted to share with you this second volume from the WFCJ network and trust that you will be fascinated and shocked with what follows. Importantly, we also hope that it will motivate you to think about, talk about and help respond to the adversities facing women and families. While this collection primarily highlights the issues facing communities in England and Wales, we acknowledge that the experiences of punishment, abuse and (in)justice will reflect many women and families beyond this jurisdiction. Therefore, we invite the reader to consider and draw links to the evidence from further afield as these findings have important international application.

The network, and as is represented in this collection, seeks to be inclusive, representing the voices of several individuals and organisations working in related fields who are passionate and dedicated to bringing about positive change. You may also notice that the research, ideas and discussions come from a range of authors (such as academics, practitioners, service users) who are at different stages of their journeys and seeking to shed light on their important work. This is still an unusual concept and practice in academic books but is something we are most proud of. We believe inclusivity and diversity are important to drive forward change which, as already mentioned, has been unimpressive and inadequate to date, and perhaps further stifled within the recent social climate. Our collaborative endeavour is, however, about the long term and so if anyone would like to join forces and contribute to the network then we would welcome you with open arms. Please do contact the editors and/or follow us on Twitter (@WomenCri1).

Finally, we are so grateful to all the contributors for their hard work and dedication to this project, particularly in the challenging times as generated by the pandemic – without them and those with whom they have engaged, this book would not be possible.

We now encourage you to absorb yourselves in the chapters that follow.

Natalie, Isla and Lucy

References

Baldwin, L. (2021) Motherhood Challenged: A Matricentric Feminist Study Exploring the Persisting Impact of Maternal Imprisonment on Maternal Identity and Role, Doctoral thesis, Leicester: De Montfort University.

Baldwin, L., Masson, I. and Booth, N. (2021) Continuing the conversation: reflections from the Women, Family, Crime and Justice network, in Masson, I., Baldwin, L. and Booth, N. (eds.), *Critical Reflections on Women, Family, Crime and Justice*, Bristol: Policy Press, pp 219–27.

Booth, N., Masson, I. and Baldwin, L. (2018) Promises, promises: can the Female Offender Strategy deliver?, *Probation Journal*, 65(4), 429–38.

Booth, N. and Masson, I. (2021) Loved ones of remand prisoners: the hidden victims of COVID-19, *Prison Service Journal*, 235, 17–31.

Casciani, D. (2021) Sarah Everard murder: Wayne Couzens given whole life sentence, BBC News, [online] 1 October. Available from: www.bbc.co.uk/news/uk-england-london-58747614 [Accessed: 6 October 2021].

Edgar, K., Harris, M., Maguire, D. and Vince, C. (2021) A CAPPTIVE snapshot of life under Covid, *Prison Service Journal*, 235, 16–22.

Food Foundation (2020) Demand for free school meals rises sharply as the economic impact of COVID-19 on families bites, [online] 12 October. Available from: https://foodfoundation.org.uk/demand-for-free-school-meals-rises-sharply-as-the-economic-impact-of-covid-19-on-families-bites/ [Accessed: 6 October 2021].

Havard, T. (2021) Domestic abuse and COVID-19: a year into the pandemic, House of Commons Library, [online] 11 May. Available from: https://commonslibrary.parliament.uk/domestic-abuse-and-covid-19-a-year-into-the-pandemic/ [Accessed: 6 October 2021].

Joint Committee on Human Rights (2020) Human Rights and the Government's Response to COVID-19: Children Whose Mothers Are in Prison, London: Joint Committee on Human Rights, [online] 3 July. Available from: https://publications.parliament.uk/pa/jt5801/jtselect/jtrights/518/51803.htm#_idTextAnchor000 [Accessed: 19 September 2020].

Konadu, K. and Gyamfi, B. (2021) Black Lives Matter: how far has the movement come? The Conversation, [online] 8 September. Available from: https://theconversation.com/black-lives-matter-how-far-has-the-movement-come-165492 [Accessed: 6 October 2021].

Masson, I., Booth, N. and Baldwin, L. (2021) Starting the conversation: an introduction to the Women, Family, Crime and Justice network, in Masson, I., Baldwin, L. and Booth, N. (eds.) Critical Reflections on Women, Family, Crime and Justice, Bristol: Policy Press, pp 1–10.

Masson, I., Baldwin, L. and Booth, N. (eds.) (2021) Critical Reflections on Women, Family, Crime and Justice, Bristol: Policy Press.

Ministry of Justice (MoJ) (2018) Female Offender Strategy, London: Ministry of Justice.

MoJ (2021) Press release: extra funding for organisations that steer women away from crime, [online] 23 January. Available from: www.gov.uk/government/news/extra-funding-for-organisations-that-steer-women-away-from-crime [Accessed: 6 October 2021].

Prison and Probation Ombudsman (2021) Independent Investigation into the Death of Baby A at HMP Bronzefield on 27 September 2019, London: Prison and Probation Ombudsman.

Prison and Probation Ombudsman (2022) Independent Investigation into the Death of Baby B at HMP&YOI Styal on 18 June 2020, London: Prison and Probation Ombudsman.

PART I

Punishing women in the criminal justice system

2

Pregnancy and new motherhood in prison during the COVID-19 pandemic

Laura Abbott

Introduction

The prison population of women in England is approximately 3,600 (Ministry of Justice [MoJ], 2021a). Women in prison are reported to have many complex issues which include enduring childhood trauma, disadvantage, homelessness, domestic violence and resultant misuse of illegal substances (Corston, 2007; Baldwin, 2015). Approximately 66 per cent of women in prison are mothers (Beresford et al, 2020; Baldwin, 2021). It is estimated that there are approximately 600 pregnancies and 100 births per year (Kennedy et al, 2016; Abbott, 2018). Of the 12 women's prisons in England and Wales six have Mother and Baby Units (MBU), with 64 MBU places available nationally (MoJ, 2021b). It is understood that around 50 per cent of babies will remain with their mothers and 50 per cent will be placed outside of prison with family or foster carers (Kennedy et al, 2016). The process of applying for an MBU place usually involves a range of multi-agency assessments, culminating in an MBU 'board' where a mother attends to give evidence of why she should be guaranteed a place with her baby.

There has been policy interest in women in prison and specifically pregnant women and mothers recently, including a new position paper published by the Royal College of Midwives (RCM, 2019) which outlines best practice for working with expectant women in prison. Following this, the MoJ (2020) published a 'Review of operational policy on pregnancy, mother and baby units and maternal separation' where additional and specific guidance around pregnancy, birth, separation and staff training was issued. Tragic deaths of two babies born to imprisoned mothers also led to investigations being launched. Findings from the first investigation found considerable concerns about the care and management of the baby's mother with a significant number of recommendations to improve maternity services (Prisons and Probation Ombudsman, 2021). It is likely further guidance will be provided, particularly in relation to the care of pregnant mothers who are not yet placed within an MBU space. Nevertheless, and despite this increased policy attention, there remain concerns about the welfare and support for this population, especially during the COVID-19 pandemic.

The chapter opens with some background of the experiences of women in English prisons, providing some research evidence in relation to pregnancy in the prison population. Descriptions of the author's research into pregnancy in prison and the pilot project into birth supporters' experiences with separated women are explained. Findings in relation to pregnant women's experiences of the COVID-19 pandemic in prison are illustrated through excerpts of birth supporters' accounts. The chapter concludes that prison was already a challenging environment for pregnant women to navigate before COVID-19, but has been brought to the fore by the pandemic.

Pregnancy in prison pre-pandemic

Despite the aforementioned estimates, it is unclear exactly how many pregnant women and new mothers are in prison in England and Wales as this is not routinely recorded (Albertson et al, 2014; Beresford, 2020). One of the earliest large-scale studies surveying the demography of pregnant women and new mothers in UK prisons was commissioned by the Home Office over 20 years ago (Caddle and Crisp, 1997). This two-stage study was considered valuable in that it was one of the earliest to profile, on a larger scale, the demographics of female prisoners. While not necessarily being able to provide 'cause and effect', surveys offer a snapshot of a moment in time (McKenna et al, 2010). Caddle and Crisp's (1997) study, although not specifically focused upon pregnancy in prison, found that 61 per cent of the 1,766 women surveyed were either pregnant or the mother of a child under the age of 18.

Another notable opportunity to learn more about the demography and experiences of female prisoners occurred when Baroness Jean Corston undertook a review of the UK female prison estate over a period of nine months following six suicides by women in one English prison (Corston, 2007). Analysis of the findings demonstrated that most women in prison were disadvantaged either through poverty, mental illness, historic abuse, addiction or ill health. It was reported that the majority of women had children, and several were pregnant. The Corston Report made 43 recommendations, taking a 'radical new approach' to improve the criminal justice system (CJS) for women. This proposal suggested a holistic stance towards imprisoned women and the opening of more community centres to use as an alternative to prison sentences (see Chapter 3 for a critical discussion about women's centres). Efforts were made to reduce the female prison population following Corston's Report, and prisoner numbers did reduce between 2007 and 2015 (MoJ, 2015). However, by 2017 only two of the 43 recommendations had been implemented, with the majority either not executed at all or only partially applied (Moore et al, 2017).

Of further concern, between the years 2015 and 2016, suicide rates in prison were reportedly the highest they had been since records began in 1978 (Baybutt and Chemlal, 2016). In 2016, 12 women committed suicide in prison, which is significantly more than when Corston first commissioned her Report into prison conditions (Doward, 2016; Prison Reform Trust, 2019). Interest was shown in the welfare of new mothers and babies in prison by the then UK Conservative government in 2016 (Brown, 2016); one prison reported the suicide of a perinatal woman, five days after the birth and subsequent removal of her third child (Parveen, 2016). Furthermore, the independent investigation into this suicide found that miscommunication and a lack of multi-disciplinary planning may have contributed to her distress (Newcomen, 2016). Likewise, inconsistency in maternity care provision in the UK was exposed by O'Keefe and Dixon (2016), while Sikand's (2017) research exposed the difficulties of gaining a place on an MBU and, if a place is denied by the 'board', the complexities of the appeal process. Baldwin and Epstein (2017) found that mothers in their study attributed the loss of their babies through miscarriage, in part, to the stress of being pregnant in prison. In the Baldwin and Epstein study two miscarriages occurred to mothers during their imprisonment, one in a mother's cell overnight and the second in an ambulance en route to hospital – this mother reported being in handcuffs throughout her miscarriage experience. Yet, this experience contrasts with guidance on the management of pregnant women which states that pregnant women should receive suitable rest and nutrition, handcuffs should not to be used and they should not travel in cellular vans (Prison Service Order 4800, 2008; Abbott et al, 2020). Given these exceptionally concerning findings, our attention now turns to the expanding academic interest in the experiences of pregnancy in prison in the UK (Davies et al, 2020), including my doctoral study (Abbott, 2018).

My doctoral ethnographic research aimed to uncover the experiences of pregnancy in prison in 2015/2016. Following a favourable ethical review, interviews with 28 women and ten members of staff, and ten months of fieldwork in three English prisons took place. Capturing the atmosphere through description and reflection gave context to the women's experiences as well as presenting the routine minutiae of prison life. The experience of pregnancy was detailed through accounts of women's entry into prison, the environmental impact, their expectations and access to necessities, the deprivations on their health and how they employed strategies to cope. The reality of health care in prison, depictions of indignity, the experience of giving birth in a prison cell and staff–prisoner relationships were all described. The main finding was that pregnancy is an incongruity within the prison system, which is chiefly designed for men, with little thought for pregnant women (Abbott, 2018).

In a later piece of writing with colleagues (Abbott et al, 2020) I developed the concept of 'institutional ignominy' whereby women experience shaming as a result of institutional practices. This study also discovered new information about how the women circumnavigate the system to negotiate entitlements. A new typology of prison officer appeared from this study: a member of prison staff who accompanies labouring women to hospital where the role of bed watch officer can become that of a birth supporter. The distressing experience of cell births was a finding from both my studies and evidence was subsequently reported to the Joint Human Rights Committee (JHRC) in 2019 during their inquiry into mothers and children affected by imprisonment. Further recommendations from the evidence include: the need for wider dissemination of the *Birth Charter* (Kennedy et al, 2016) which offers appropriate and evidence-based guidance, and a unified alliance between the Prison Service, National Health Service (NHS) Trusts and charities to facilitate the support of pregnant women.

Before COVID-19, research demonstrated that prison was already an unhealthy and unsafe place for pregnancies (Abbott, 2018; Davies et al, 2020). The experience of being locked in prison cells is representative of the prison experience, and my research (Abbott, 2018) showed that this caused a claustrophobic sensation for some pregnant women. With pregnancy as a standpoint, being locked in prison cells generated feelings of anxiety and discomfort. For instance, several participants were locked behind the cell door all day, especially in their latter stages, due to being unable to work. The feelings of isolation led to claustrophobia and concerns about being locked in alone during labour. In my doctoral study (Abbott, 2018, p 70) one mother said: "I get panic attacks, and I start getting them when I'm closed in. ... If I'm in a slow labour I'm going to be locked behind my door, that's my only worry" (Tamsin). Being locked in also made the physiological symptoms of pregnancy, such as morning sickness, harder to manage. Another mother reported: "I needed to be sick, and every time I have to beg to have my door open, so I can go to the toilet" (Abi).

Being behind a cell door when pregnant has also led to the worst of outcomes. A baby died in prison in June 2020 – the mother was serving a relatively short sentence and neither she nor the prison knew she was pregnant. However, it is reported that the woman was not referred for medical attention despite repeated calls because of the pain she was experiencing (Taylor, 2020). Given these experiences, pregnancy, even if unknown, should remain a consideration for women of childbearing age, until it is possible to rule this out. This is especially important given the vulnerabilities women bring with them to prison, such as substance misuse. It is because of these circumstances that in the conclusion of my doctorate, I argued that: 'Women should not be giving birth in prison cells and if, on a rare occasion, an unexpected birth occurs, the minimum she should expect is to have an appropriately-trained professional to support her and her baby' (Abbott, 2018, p 181).

However, there remain inconsistencies across prisons in England (Abbott, 2018). This has been despite the importance of antenatal preparation to learn about labour, birth and the options for women having been a recommendation from research with demonstrable excellent outcomes both inside and outside of the prison environment (Baldwin, 2018; Barimani et al, 2018). Caddle and Crisp's (1997) study found that from the 63 women interviewed who were pregnant, the majority had not attended antenatal preparation classes. Provision of antenatal classes in prison remains ad hoc and they are usually led by charities, such as Birth Companions[1] who are currently supporting women in three UK prisons. Women who had access to such classes reported feeling more content with the quality of care provision (Kennedy et al, 2016). Following the wider sector supporting women involved in the CJS, trauma-informed approaches (TIAs[2]) have been implemented by practitioners who work with pregnant women in prison (Delap, 2021). For instance, Birth Companions apply a TIA to the antenatal groups they lead in prison, with the director of the charity (Delap, 2021, p 74) explaining how they work: 'to identify women's experiences of trauma and offer targeted support where appropriate to address the issues that have been disclosed'.

Despite some positive changes concerning pregnancy and prison following the aforementioned increased academic and policy attention, the situation during the COVID-19 pandemic brought about new challenges. Research into pregnant women's experiences during the pandemic is yet to materialise but, coming from a perspective that being locked in was already a cause of great stress, it is important to reflect upon the specific adversities experienced by imprisoned pregnant women during this time. Not only can this enable lessons to be learnt for future pandemics, but it furthers the much-needed conversations and considerations about the impact of imprisonment for pregnant women.

Prison health care during COVID-19 and its impact on pregnant women

Before reviewing prison health care during COVID-19, it is important to explain how, in the UK, there is statutory recognition that all prisoners should receive an equivalence of health care to that provided in the community (Council of Europe, 2006). Health care for prisoners is provided through the NHS. Economically, responsibility for health funding lies with the Department of Health (DH) and the Strategic Health Authorities (SHAs). More recently, private health care providers such as Care UK™ have been contracted as providers of prison health care for 21 prisons in England and Wales (Plimmer, 2016). Furthermore, the United Nations (UN) Bangkok

Rules (2013) state that women in prison should be given gender-specific care (UN, 2013). Article 3 of the Human Rights Act (UN General Assembly, 1948) has a strong legal basis in the UK, and every woman has the right to make decisions about her body during pregnancy and to receive respectful treatment (Schiller, 2016; O'Malley, Baldwin and Abbott, 2021). Davies et al (2020) reported on prison health care prior to the pandemic and found that 22 per cent of midwifery appointments were missed compared with 14 per cent in the general population, and that as many as 10 per cent of women ended up giving birth in their cells. This indicates some significant issues in the provision of health care services to pregnant women even before COVID-19. However, while health care in UK prisons was maintained during COVID-19 (NHS England, 2021) a number of restrictions and changes, including staffing levels, the lack of testing and vaccination, all impacted on the way care was delivered (HM Inspectorate of Prisons, 2021).

NHS England (2021) maintained prison health care during the pandemic, adapting to a more virtual way of working in order to ensure continuity of care. HM Inspectorate of Prisons (2021) reported that adaptations included minimising face-to-face meetings in favour of virtual ones and limiting movement around prisons. The report goes on to explain that the outcomes of these changes was often that prisoners reported a lack of communication in relation to health care requirements, increased waiting times and delays in getting medication. This was a cause of distress for some prisoners and likely formed even more barriers to medical support for pregnant women during the pandemic. At the start of COVID-19, pregnant women were asked to shield (Kmietowicz, 2020). In prison this translated to women being let out of cells at separate times from the main population, and spending the majority of a 24-hour period locked in their cells. Women housed on the MBUs with their babies could be in a support bubble. In the earlier stages of the vaccine roll-out pregnant women were not eligible so had to continue to shield away from the main prison population. This may have led to further feelings of isolation and fear, or could have been a comfort for some. Moreover, in line with wider changes to health care delivery, support from charities such as Birth Companions was also adapted to be provided via email or telephone. Tragically, during COVID-19, two babies were stillborn with damning investigation findings (Prison and Probation Ombudsman, 2022).

Importantly, the enforced isolation pregnant and new mothers in prison experienced will also undoubtedly have had an impact on babies living within the MBU space. Many did not get to meet their fathers or other relatives outside due to the restrictions and cessation of visits at this time (Children Heard and Seen, 2020). This caused difficulty for pre-verbal young children and babies due to prolonged separation from their parent with no understanding of what was happening (Minson, 2021). Research into the needs and experiences of pregnant women and new mothers in contact with the CJS by Clinks and Birth Companions (2021) reported on the impact of the pandemic. They found that appropriate and timely access to support was lacking through 'digital exclusion' exacerbating the stigma experienced by women. Although purple visits (virtual visits via video link) in some establishments commenced, the report suggested that this did not appear to consider small infants and/or babies, and exacerbated anxieties of mothers separated from their children. The importance of multi-agency and partnership working was a main recommendation of this report following feedback from women that when this worked well, their experience was much improved and more consistent, placing the woman as central to care and support provided.

However, these poor and punitive prison experiences might have been avoided for pregnant women. At the start of the pandemic there were calls for MBU mothers and pregnant women to be released from prison due to safety concerns. Dr Shona Minson and I released a short film (Minson and Abbott, 2020) about the impact upon sentencing pregnant women to prison. Campaigning and calling upon the government with powerful allies in parliament and media, we worked hard with our charity partners to ensure the early release of pregnant women. Sadly, there were very few releases due to the caveats of who could and who could not be released in terms of their offence, alongside post-release accommodation challenges. Only 253 prisoners were released under COVID-19 temporary release schemes, 21 of those pregnant women (Beard, 2020). Given the high numbers ineligible for release, qualitative research into women in prison during COVID-19, including expectant mothers, is therefore a priority for future enquiries. Indeed, there has never been a more important time to examine pregnancy in prisons through a COVID-19 lens and the research presented in this chapter intends to shed some light on these experiences.

Methods

This chapter is based on post-doctoral research which was undertaken as a pilot study in preparation for a larger-scale qualitative research project exploring the experiences of pregnant women and new mothers being mandatorily separated from their babies while in prison. The pilot study objectives were to uncover themes and elucidate the experiences of those who support women being separated from their newborn babies to add to the secondary analysis of women's experiences of separation while in prison. Favourable ethical opinion was granted by the University of Hertfordshire.[3] The audio-recorded, qualitative, in-depth interviews were undertaken virtually with 12 women who provide, or who have provided, pregnancy and birth support to women in prison who are or were being separated from their babies in the UK. The sample included volunteers and practitioners who support pregnant women in the CJS. The decision to collect data virtually was guided by COVID-19, but it also provided an opportunity to ask about COVID-19 conditions for women and revealed some important preliminary findings. Thematic analysis was used to analyse the data and three themes are presented and discussed next.

Findings

This section includes anonymised extracts from interviews with pregnancy and birth supporters from the pilot study. Pseudonyms have been assigned to protect anonymity. Participants reported a number of concerns for pregnant women and new mothers during COVID-19. Key themes explored in this chapter relate to: 1) Mental health versus physical risk of COVID-19; 2) Support and virtual decision making; and 3) Being released into the COVID-19 world. Of importance, many of these themes build on my doctoral research findings (Abbott, 2018) showing how issues intensified during COVID-19; where our knowledge has expanded is highlighted in the discussions that follow.

Mental health versus physical risk of COVID-19

The risks to mental health during COVID-19 were well evidenced for the prison population (Pfefferbaum and North, 2020). Existing literature suggests that women in prison are already at high risk of poor mental health, often due to enduring multiple trauma (Corston, 2007; Prison Reform Trust, 2019), and that pregnancy and motherhood can also increase vulnerabilities to mental health issues (North et al, 2006; Baldwin, 2021). As such, the impact of the pandemic on imprisoned pregnant women and new mothers was an issue that several birth supporters described:

> 'the cost to their mental and emotional health, which is often compromised anyway, versus the real risk of COVID, and how would, how harmful that would be. But, again, a lot of these women do have complex medical needs as well for themselves, so they are already considered vulnerable, it's difficult.' (Jasmine, birth supporter)

Many of the services usually provided for pregnant women and new mothers had been withdrawn suddenly due to the COVID-19-enforced national lockdown. The reduction in support was also noted as a potential issue for exacerbating poor mental health. This was a concern for birth supporters who worried about the women they usually visited on a weekly, face-to-face basis (Clinks and Birth Companions, 2021). While private, wing-based phone contact was enabled through the prisons facilitating Birth Companion's support, one supporter described the challenges of continuity of care for pregnant women, providing an example of the impact on one mother she was supporting remotely:

'I think lack of support, no one coming into the prison, and not being able to access things, she said that she really needed to speak to someone, she said they're just – there's no one in the prison. You can put an app[4] in, but nobody is. … This was – actually, this was in full lockdown, so this is back in late spring and summer [in 2020]. So, she was all over the place, upset, angry, frustrated.' (Blossom, birth supporter)

It is understood that during COVID-19 women were receiving health care in prison. Baldwin and Epstein (2017), Abbott et al, (2020) and Baldwin and Abbott (2021) suggest that inequality in health care for pregnant women was already an issue. This leads to a question of whether the standards of health care were equivalent to those receiving health care in the community. According to the emerging evidence from the pilot study, gaps in health care equivalence worsened during the pandemic. Consequently, some birth supporters reported that women had deteriorating episodes of self-harm:

'I'm sure COVID conditions is contributing to her poor mental health at the moment, so it's very concerning, really. I think she's struggling with self-harm; I think that is one of the factors. I know she is having support from the health care team at [Prison X]. But I don't – and this is probably mainly COVID-related – I don't think she is getting any kind of specialist therapeutic support to help her with the separation.' (Rose, birth supporter)

Several participants in my earlier research (Abbott, 2018) conveyed feelings of isolation and claustrophobia when they were locked in their cells towards the latter end of pregnancy, reporting panic attacks, fear and exacerbating physical discomforts. Worsening self-harm and exacerbations in poor mental health have been reported across the prison population since the start of the global pandemic and subsequent lockdowns in prison (Hewson et al, 2021). Taken together, this may explain why the birth supporters in this pilot study felt powerless in wanting to be able to do more to support the women in prison. During the COVID-19 pandemic pregnant women were shielding, meaning they would spend most of their time behind their door, in their cells. One birth supporter described what she had heard was happening inside prison:

'They are locked up for 23 and a half hours a day … I heard of some places that have got an hour and 15 for everything … I've heard this from peer supporters,[5] who have been in prison throughout COVID, and then peer supporters who have been released in COVID, that it was half an hour to shower and make any phone calls, and to do any exercise.' (Lily, birth supporter)

Resonant with my doctoral research (Abbott, 2018), it was found that where women reported being locked in for many hours at a time, this exacerbated the physiological symptoms of pregnancy, such as morning sickness. Anxiety was an issue for women, especially at night-time when there was a fear of being locked in as labour started. The importance of understanding the psychological and physical impact for pregnant women of lengthy times locked behind a cell door cannot be underestimated.

Virtual support and decision making

There are usually many third-sector organisations who offer face-to-face support for women in prison. Birth Companions and the Born Inside project[6] are two organisations who were unable to provide the face-to-face weekly support to incarcerated pregnant women and new mothers. This included pregnancy groups where women get together and learnt about labour and birth. It was clear from my doctoral research (Abbott, 2018) that, often, women, especially those in their first pregnancy, had no accurate information about key aspects of the process. For instance, this may include what happens at the onset of labour, birthing options and choices. The groups that provided these services pre-COVID-19 were invaluable to the women as they learnt of birth options such as pain relief, infant feeding, mobility in labour and an opportunity to meet with other pregnant women. The importance of pregnancy groups in prison have been described by women receiving support from the charity Birth Companions, with evaluations of the services reporting how positive reviews consist of statements such as: 'feeling like a normal pregnant woman' (Kennedy et al, 2016, p 25). Another key purpose of the pregnancy groups which was lost during the pandemic was the opportunity for women to demonstrate to social services their motivation to care for their baby. Therefore, this may have led to more post-birth mother–child separations, as one supporter explained:

> 'Services weren't running, like the groups and things, nothing was running, so how were women supposed to demonstrate that they've done. … They would ask for information, oh, can you send me a course I can do in the cell? You're pregnant, you're carrying, you know the likelihood of you being separated is very high, but you feel powerless to do anything within your control, because nothing is within your control at that particular point.' (Leilani, birth supporter)

The decisions around whether women could remain with their baby were undertaken virtually through MBU prison board panels during COVID-19. Birth supporters described how women felt penalised as they had been unable to demonstrate that they had the parenting skills to keep their baby:

'I think COVID just brings home any additional challenges, I think around the information and being able to engage positively with the child protection process, like a lot of women that we've been engaging with pre-proceedings. And trying to do that in the prison was impossible, in a community it was hard enough, but at least in the community, social workers could have Skype, zoom equivalent kind of conversations with women, and do assessments or similar over that kind of medium. In the prison, there was no opportunity to do that and women felt really aggrieved by that, and justifiably, because they were like, well, I'm being denied the opportunity to participate in a process which is actually life changing for me and my baby. But they can't arrange a video call, they can't arrange – it felt like a lot more weight was placed on old history, because they hadn't been able to evidence, satisfactorily, that degree of change, that kind of what they're looking for.' (Cassia, birth supporter)

It has been documented that there have been delays to court processes because of COVID-19 (Bannon and Keith, 2021; Song and Legg, 2021). Furthermore, this has meant that women may have spent longer remanded in prison waiting for a trial or for release (HM Courts and Tribunals Service, 2020; Booth and Masson, 2021). Some participants reflected on this and the impact it may have had on the women and the Prison Service in general: "During this last year, I think the courts have probably worked very slowly. And I think there possibly has been an effort not to convict too many, because of the special circumstances" (Rose, birth supporter). Birth supporters would not usually submit evidence to the board and/or be with the women during this process. However, much of the understanding about the decision-making process has come from supporting women. The lack of provision of face-to-face support during COVID-19 indicates reduced knowledge about the transparency and the fairness of these decision-making processes, from the woman and birth supporter's perspective.

In an application process that was already problematic (Sikand, 2017), the added difficulties in making important decisions about whether a baby can reside with his/her mother on an MBU via a virtual format in prison has not yet been explored. It was also noted by one birth supporter how the complexities of the service working in a joined-up way may have been undermined because of COVID-19:

'And often, again, if you think of like the lack of continuity in so many of our services, it is this kind of snapshot of this woman has done X, Y and Z. And it's very much a kind of an on-paper report, and I guess during COVID that's been exacerbated, because people this kind of snapshot image of how well women have been doing, because they can't see them face to face. Yeah, it's complicated. I know that women are sitting boards, but because we've not been in the prison, I suspect other members of staff might have a fuller picture of how those boards are happening. But I don't know, personally, how the boards are happening right now.' (Alyssa, birth supporter)

Participants were concerned about the lack of consistency and transparency in the processes of evaluating women and their suitability for a place on an MBU via virtual formats:

'It felt like authorities had been quite reactionary, and quite quick to make decisions based on the papers perhaps, rather than having a ... Like getting to know a woman, like actually having more than one phone call with her to get a sense of who she is, and what she's about. Which I don't know how – if we're not to actively be able to participate in a process, feels really cruel and unfair, because it's not ... That doesn't feel just to me, particularly when the stakes are so high that they can't, they were unable to fully engage, or the decisions were made before women were given the opportunity to demonstrate that.' (Cassia, birth supporter)

There were clearly anxieties about the processes on behalf of the women who were being supported. The sense of frustration in a system which was complex prior to COVID-19 (O'Keefe and Dixon, 2016; Sikand, 2017) was exacerbated because of the pandemic locking down most of the face-to-face arrangements. One participant described the situation of a woman recently mandatorily separated from her baby:

'She felt that she'd been further penalised by the situation of lockdown and that she hasn't had the support that she'd been promised, a parenting assessment in the community ... because of the situation that hadn't happened. She didn't feel really satisfied with their justification, and why that hadn't happened.' (Jasmine, birth supporter)

There was some resignation that the situation was unavoidable, due to public concerns and managing the risks of COVID-19 spread, owing to public health concerns. However, the recognition of the impact upon a woman's psychological wellbeing when separated from her child(ren) was a concern:

'Things may have fallen back in terms of the way things are having to work at the moment, through no fault of anyone's, other than the situation. But it's even more important, that the women are getting the support they need psychologically and that that's provided within the prison setting, even if they can't go out and visit babies, or see family or get that other kind of contact ... I don't know how the prisons are dealing with all of that.' (Lily, birth supporter)

The findings from my past research (Abbott, 2018) demonstrated that prison staff opinions centred on missed opportunities for women to change and become a good parent, suggesting that women should be given the opportunity to parent their babies when, often, the baby would be removed. The suggestion from Lily that progress made more recently with guidance from the *Birth Charter* (Birth Companions, 2016), for example, is being undermined appears concerning, especially when conditions were already challenging for pregnant women.

Women who had been granted a place on an MBU during the pandemic were enabled to form a support bubble. According to birth supporters, there were very few women housed in the MBUs, making up a small support bubble: "I think they're quite close, and they're supporting each other; and they're not being locked up, because they're in a bubble. So, I think that's been quite good for them, in terms of the rest of the prison" (Cassia, birth supporter). I have previously demonstrated that boredom was common for pregnant women pre-COVID-19 (Abbott, 2018), and some women longed to get back to the main prison as they missed their friends. Although for others, being pregnant in the main prison made some women feel vulnerable and unsafe (Abbott, 2018; Baldwin, 2021). The anxieties of being a new mother on an MBU were exacerbated by the milieu with the noises, atmosphere, post-natal emotions and having to cope with a new baby. However, the MBU environment during COVID-19 may have been a safer, more positive place for women and their babies.

Being released into the global pandemic community

Pre-COVID-19, women who had been released often focused upon their own inner strength and how they coped (Abbott, 2018). These findings demonstrated the extraordinary use of restraint and resilience in order to survive. The current evidence suggests that challenges facing women being released into the COVID-19 world were exacerbated. Several participants reflected upon the experiences of women being released into the community under COVID-19 restrictions. One birth supporter reflected on the amount of information women needed to be aware of on release:

'There was so much with COVID to take on board, so we did a lot of work preparing her ... with information. [Such as] "this place is open. This is where you can go for drug and alcohol support. Someone's going to phone you on the second day you're released"

... we facilitated all of that kind of support, and a parenting course so that she could try and build her case to have her baby returned to her.' (Lily, birth supporter)

A birth supporter described a situation where a woman had lost her place on an MBU and had her baby removed in the process during COVID-19 and was subsequently released from prison. She described the limited support offered and a lack of joined-up working between services:

'The support within the prison for her current situation, having lost her MBU place, was minimal, if nothing, and that she hadn't been able to connect with services like drug and alcohol services. She hadn't been able to connect with them. And then what I did was I supported her on her journey when she was then released on home detention curfew, so she did get out during COVID.' (Poppy, birth supporter)

It was often the birth supporter who helped the woman on release from prison. Clinks and Birth Companions (2021) call for a consistent, multi-agency approach for all women who are in contact with the CJS, with their new 'window of opportunity' research providing evidence of the importance for caring for mothers post-release. Baldwin's (2021) research highlights the need for post-release support accounting for motherhood and the maternal role/identity. Yet, there were additional challenges for mothers in preparing their babies to go into an outside world they had not yet seen. Previous accompanied trips out and weekends out for babies had all been stopped – so for many babies they had only ever seen the handful of staff on the MBU and their mothers. Also, there appears to be a reliance on the charity third sector to provide the support needed. However, charities rely mainly upon raising funds themselves, which leaves organisations vulnerable to closure, unlike public services (Power, 2021). Recommendations include cohesive partnership working across the services so that women are consistently signposted to the support and services they may need.

Conclusion

This chapter has highlighted some of the issues for pregnant women in prison and described the situation as the global pandemic took hold in 2020. This was achieved by drawing on the narratives of pregnancy supporters who were, or had been, providing support to incarcerated pregnant women and new mothers in the UK. Even before the particularly challenging time brought about by COVID-19, the complexity of women's health needs while pregnant in prison has been a constant conclusion from research and reviews (Corston, 2007; Albertson et al, 2014; Shaw et al, 2015; Baldwin, 2017; Abbott, 2018). A key finding from my doctoral research (Abbott, 2018) demonstrated that breaches of pregnant women's rights were being experienced on multiple levels, while Davies et al (2020) reported issues with accessing health care in prison while pregnant. Given this context, it is important that research explores how COVID-19 has impacted on pregnant prisoners and their babies.

To begin to bridge this gap, this chapter has drawn upon a pilot study which has included views of what happened to pregnant women during the pandemic. A key conclusion has been that the removal of face-to-face visits and the support of outside agencies has had an impact upon the psychological wellbeing of women and arguably their babies. This needs to be evaluated further and considered for the future as the repercussions could result in serious long-term harm. Charity support should continue face to face and be part of essential health care, especially considering the evidence relating to mental health. It was clear how the move to 'virtual' support was not effective for this particularly vulnerable population. The support from charities like Birth Companions increases the safety and wellbeing for women and their babies and offers a conduit between health care and trauma-informed supportive care that women value intensely. Sadly, opportunities for this to help alleviate struggles and concerns experienced by expectant and new mothers during COVID-19 were lost both in prison and as women prepared for release. Of course, this is not to lay blame with these charities but, on the contrary, to fully appreciate the importance of their work. As such, lessons do need to be learnt from this pandemic, especially in light of the outcomes for pregnant women and new mothers in prison. This includes consideration of how releasing women from a lockdown prison into a lockdown world may look for them and their babies. Finally, while the new empirical findings shared in this chapter begin to shed light on the complexities of the COVID-19 situation for imprisoned pregnant women, further qualitative research with women's experiences at the forefront of future enquiries is necessary.

Reflection points

The following points are for the reader to consider when reflecting on the experiences of incarcerated pregnant women and new mothers.

- How and in what ways might timely support be offered to pregnant women, new mothers and their babies in prisons during a pandemic?
- What special circumstances should be taken into account when life-changing decisions are being made (such as the removal of a baby from their mother)?

- How can virtual and online communications be used more effectively in prisons to support pregnant women and new mothers?
- Consider ways to support the provision of consistent, multi-agency support for women that is trauma-informed.

Notes

[1] For more information about Birth Companions, see www.birthcompanions.org.uk/
[2] See Goddard (2021) in reference list for more information about TIAs.
[3] 30 July 2021, Protocol number: HSK/SF/UH/04236.
[4] The word 'app' means general application. An app is a form available for prisoners to make general requests to the prison (for example, a doctor's appointment).
[5] Peer supporters provide emotional and social support to others who share a lived experience. In this case, women in prison who have experienced pregnancy, supporting pregnant women in prison.
[6] For more information about the Born Inside project, see www.mariamontessori.org/outreach/born-inside/

References

Abbott, L. (2018) The Incarcerated Pregnancy: An Ethnographic Study of Perinatal Women in English Prisons, Doctoral thesis in Health Research, Hatfield: University of Hertfordshire.

Abbott, L., Scott, T., Thomas, H. and Weston, K. (2020) Pregnancy and childbirth in English prisons: institutional ignominy and the pains of imprisonment, *Sociology of Health & Illness*, 42(3), 660–75.

Albertson, K., O'Keefe, C., Burke, C., Lessing-Turner, G. and Renfrew, M. (2014) Addressing health inequalities for mothers and babies in prison: health and inequality, *Applying Public Health Research to Policy and Practice*, 16, 39– 47.

Baldwin, L. (2015) *Mothering Justice: Working with Mothers in Criminal and Social Justice Settings*, Hampshire: Waterside Press.

Baldwin, L. (2018) Motherhood disrupted: reflections of post-prison mothers. *Emotion, Space and Society*, 26, 49–56.

Baldwin, L. (2021) *Motherhood Challenged: A Matricentric Feminist Study Exploring the Persisting Impact of Maternal Imprisonment on Maternal Identity and Role*, Leicester: De Montfort University.

Baldwin, L. and Abbott, L. (2021) Incarcerated motherhood: reflecting on 100 years of imprisoning mothers. *Prison Service Journal*, 257, 29–38.

Baldwin, L. and Epstein, R. (2017) Short but Not Sweet: A Study of the Imposition of Short Custodial Sentences on Women, and in Particular, on Mothers, Leicester: De Montfort University.

Bannon, A.L. and Keith, D. (2021) Remote court: principles for virtual proceedings during the COVID-19 pandemic and beyond, *Northwestern University Law Review*, 115(6), 1875–920.

Barimani, M., Forslund Frykedal, K., Rosander, M., and Berlin, A. (2018) Childbirth and parenting preparation in antenatal classes, *Midwifery*, 57, 1–7, doi: 10.1016/j.midw.2017.10.021.

Baybutt, M. and Chemlal, K. (2016) Health-promoting prisons: theory to practice, *Global Health Promotion*, 23(1), 66–74.

Beard, J. (2020) Coronavirus: prisons (England and Wales) briefing paper, House of Commons Library, [online], 18 May. Available from: https://researchbriefings.files.parliament.uk/documents/CBP-8892/CBP-8892.pdf [Accessed: 31 August 2021].

Beresford, S., Earle, J., Loucks, N. and Pinkman, A. (2020) 'What about me?' The impact on children when mothers are involved in the criminal justice system. Mothering from the inside, London: Prison Reform Trust. Available from: https://prisonreformtrust.org.uk/publication/what-about-me-the-impact-on-children-when-mothers-are-involved-in-the-criminal-justice-system/ [Accessed: 27 January 2023].

Booth, N. and Masson, I. (2021) Loved ones of remand prisoners: the hidden victims of COVID-19, *Prison Service Journal*, 253, 23–31.

Brown, D. (2016) Finding diamonds in the rough and helping them shine: prospects for penal reform in the UK, *Alternative Law Journal*, 41(3), 155.

Birth Companions (2016) Birth Charter for women in prisons in England and Wales. Available from: https://www.birthcompanions.org.uk/resources/5-birth-charter-for-women-in-prison-in-england-and-wales [Accessed: 16 February 2023].

Caddle, D. and Crisp, D. (1997) *Home Office Research Study 162: Imprisoned Women and Mothers*, London: Home Office.

Corston, J. (2007) *The Corston Report: A Report by Baroness Jean Corston of a Review of Women with Particular Vulnerabilities in the Criminal Justice System: The Need for a Distinct, Radically Different, Visibly-Led, Strategic, Proportionate, Holistic, Woman-Centred, Integrated Approach*, London: Home Office.

Council of Europe Committee of Ministers (2006) European prison rules, Recommendation Rec. 2 of the Committee of Ministers to Member States on the European Prison Rules.

Children Heard and Seen (2020) Life in lockdown, [online]. Available from: http://childrenheardandseen.co.uk/2020/10/08/life-in-lockdown-2020-report/ [Accessed: 27 September 2021].

Clinks and Birth Companions (2021) A window of opportunity: understanding the needs and experiences of pregnant women and new mothers in the criminal justice system in the community, [online] 24 May. Available from: www.clinks.org/publication/window-opportunity [Accessed: 1 June 2021].

Davies, M., Rolewicz, L., Schlepper, L. and Fagunwa, F. (2020) Locked out? Prisoners' use of hospital care, Research report, Nuffield Trust. Available from: https://www.nuffieldtrust.org.uk/files/2022-08/1614850952-prisoners-use-of-hospital-services-main-report.pdf [Accessed 16 February 2023].

Delap, N. (2021) Trauma-informed care of perinatal women, in Abbott, L. (ed.) *Complex Social Issues and the Perinatal Woman*, Cham: Springer, pp 15–33.

Doward, J. (2016) New crisis in prisons as suicides hit record levels, *The Guardian*, [online], 29 October. Available from: www.theguardian.com/society/2016/oct/29/prison-suicides-record-levels-scandal [Accessed: 5 October 2020].

Goddard, A. (2021) Adverse childhood experiences and trauma-informed care, *Journal of Pediatric Health Care*, 35(2), 145–55.

Hewson, T., Green, R., Shepherd, A., Hard, J. and Shaw, J. (2021) The effects of COVID-19 on self-harm in UK prisons, *BJPsych Bulletin*, 45(3), 131–3.

HM Courts and Tribunals Service (2020) COVID-19: overview of HMCTS response, [online], July. Available from: https://assets.publishing.service.gov.uk/government/uploads/system/uploads/attachment_data/file/896779/HMCTS368_recovery_-_COVID-19-_Overview_of_HMCTS_response_A4L_v3.pdf [Accessed: 28 September 2021].

HM Inspectorate of Prisons (2021) What happens to prisoners in a pandemic?, [online], 11 February. Available from: www.justiceinspectorates.gov.uk/hmiprisons/inspections/what-happens-to-prisoners-in-a-pandemic/ [Accessed: 27 September 2021].

Kennedy, A., Marshall, D., Parkinson, D., Delap, N. and Abbott, L. (2016) *Birth Charter for Women in Prison in England and Wales*, London: Birth Companions.

Kmietowicz, Z. (2020) Covid-19: highest risk patients are asked to stay at home for 12 weeks, *British Medical Journal*, 268, DOI: https://doi.org/10.1136/bmj.m1170.

McKenna, H., Hasson, F. and Keeney, S. (2010) Surveys, in Gerrish, K. and Lacey, A. (eds.) *The Research Process in Nursing*, New Jersey: John Wiley & Sons, pp 216–36.

Ministry of Justice (MoJ) (2015) *Statistics on Women and the Criminal Justice System 2015: A Ministry of Justice Publication under Section 95 of the Criminal Justice Act 1991*, [online]. Available from: https://assets.publishing.service.gov.uk/government/uploads/system/uploads/attachment_data/file/572043/women-and-the-criminal-justice-system-statistics-2015.pdf [Accessed: 13 October 2021].

MoJ (2020) *Review of Operational Policy on Pregnancy, Mother and Baby Units and Maternal Separation: Summary Report of the Review of PSI 49/2014 and Operational Policy on Pregnancy and Women Separated from Children Under 2 in Prison*, [online]. Available from: https://assets.publishing.service. gov.uk/government/uploads/system/uploads/attachment_data/file/905 559/summary-report-of-review-of-policy-on-mbu.pdf [Accessed: 27 September 2021].

MoJ (2021a) *Population and Capacity Briefing for Friday 16th July 2021*, London: Ministry of Justice.

MoJ (2021b) Prisons with mother and baby units, [online]. Available from: www.gov.uk/life-in-prison/pregnancy-and-childcare-in-prison [Accessed: 27 September 2021].

Minson, S. and Abbott, L. (2020) The impact of imprisonment on pregnant women and their unborn children, [online]. Available from: https:// www.independent.co.uk/news/uk/politics/pregnant-women-prison- coronavirus-covid-19-england-wales-a9416991.html [Accessed: 27 September 2021].

Minson, S. (2021) The impact of COVID-19 prison lockdowns on children with a parent in prison, University of Oxford, [online] March. Available from: www.law.ox.ac.uk/sites/files/oxlaw/the_impact_of_co vid-19_prison_lockdowns_on_children_with_a_parent_in_prison.pdf [Accessed: 13 October 2021].

Moore, L., Scraton, P. and Wahidin, A. (2017) *Women's Imprisonment and the Case for Abolition: Critical Reflections on Corston Ten Years On*, Abingdon: Routledge.

Newcomen, N. (2016) *Independent Investigation into the Death of Ms Michelle Barnes, a Prisoner at HMP Low Newton on 16 December 2015*, Prisons and Probation Ombudsman Report.

NHS (2021) Action required to tackle health inequalities in latest phase of COVID-19 response and recovery, [online]. Available from: www. england.nhs.uk/about/equality/equality-hub/action-required-to-tackle- health-inequalities-in-latest-phase-of-covid-19-response-and-recovery/ [Accessed: 11 June 2021].

North, J., Chase, L. and Alliance, M. (2006) *Getting It Right: Services for Pregnant Women, New Mothers, and Babies in Prison*, London: Lankelly Chase.

O'Keefe, C., and Dixon, L., (2016) Enhancing Care for Childbearing Women and Their Babies in Prison. Sheffield Hallam Centre for Community Justice. Available from: https://www.barrowcadbury.org. uk/wp-content/uploads/2015/12/FINAL-MBUreport-7th-December- 2015.pdf [Accessed: 16 February 2023].

O'Malley, S., Baldwin, L. and Abbott, L. (2021) Starting life in prison: reflections of the UK and Irish contexts of pregnant and new mothers in prison, through a children's rights lens, in Donson, F. and Parks, A. (eds.) *Presenting a Children's Rights Approach to Parental Imprisonment*, London: Palgrave Macmillan, pp 87–112.

Parveen, N. (2016) Prisons ombudsman investigates death of new mother taken off suicide watch, *The Guardian*, [online] 9 February. Available from: www.theguardian.com/society/2016/feb/09/new-mother-killed-herself-prison-shortly-after-taken-off-suicide-watch?CMP=share_btn_gp [Accessed: 2 January 2017].

Pfefferbaum, B. and North, C.S. (2020) Mental health and the COVID-19 pandemic, *New England Journal of Medicine*, 383(6), 510–12.

Plimmer, G. (2016) Care UK, the private equity-owned healthcare provider, becomes biggest jail healthcare provider in Britain, *Financial Times*, [online]. Available from: https://www.ft.com/content/c3b44066-1390-11e6-91da-096d89bd2173 [Accessed: 16 February 2023].

Power, E. (2021) 'Without it you're lost': examining the role and challenges of family engagement services in prisons, in Masson, I., Baldwin, L. and Booth, N. (eds.) *Critical Reflections on Women, Family, Crime and Justice*, Bristol: Policy Press, pp 153–72.

Prisons and Probation Ombudsman (PPO) (2021) Investigation into baby death at HMP Bronzefield identified key failings, [online] 22 September. Available from: https://s3-eu-west-2.amazonaws.com/ppo-prod-stor age-1g9rkhjhkjmgw/uploads/2021/09/Prisons-and-Probation-Ombuds man-Bronzefield-Baby-A-Release.pdf [Accessed: 13 October 2021].

PPO (2022) Independent investigation into the death of Baby B at HMP and YOI Styal, 18 June, London: PPO.

Prison Reform Trust (2019) *Bromley Briefings. Prison: The Facts. Summer 2019*, London: Prison Reform Trust.

Prison Service Order (PSO) 4800 (2008) *Women Prisoners*. London: Ministry of Justice.

Royal College of Midwives (2019) Position statement: perinatal women in the criminal justice system, [online]. Available from: https://uhra.herts.ac.uk/bitstream/handle/2299/21896/Perinatal_women_in_the_Crimi nal_Justice_System_7_1_.pdf?sequence=1 [Accessed: 1 May 2021].

Schiller, R. (2016) *Why Human Rights in Childbirth Matter*, London: Pinter and Martin.

Shaw, J., Downe, S. and Kingdon, C. (2015) Systematic mixed-methods review of interventions, outcomes and experiences for imprisoned pregnant women, *Journal of Advanced Nursing*, 71(7), 1451–63.

Sikand, M. (2017). *Lost Spaces: Is the Current Provision for Women Prisoners to Gain a Place in a Prison Mother and Baby Unit Fair and Accessible?* The Griffins Society, Institute of Criminology, University of Cambridge.

Song, A. and Legg, M. (2021) The courts, the remote hearing and the pandemic: from action to reflection, *University of New South Wales Law Journal*, 44(1), 126–66.

UN General Assembly (1948) *The Universal Declaration of Human Rights. Resolution Adopted by the General Assembly 10/12*, New York: United Nations.

United Nations (2013) The Bangkok rules, [online]. Available from: www. penalreform.org/priorities/women-in-the-criminal-justice-system/bang kok-rules-2/ [Accessed: 21 May 2021].

3

Empowerment or punishment? The curious case of women's centres

Gemma Ahearne

Introduction

This chapter discusses the paradox of women's centres: are they there to 'empower' or to punish? 'Women's centres are specialist community support services for women facing multiple disadvantages, including women involved in (or at risk of involvement in) the criminal justice system [CJS]' (Women's Budget Group [WBG], 2020, p 3). Women's centres have existed since the 1970s and there are estimated to be around 50 such centres in England and Wales (Tavistock Institute, 2019). The nature of funding for women's centres is that of instability; very few have any permanent funding and are thus reliant on winning bids and grants (WBG, 2020). This results in precarity for the workers, and, more importantly, inconsistency for women attending the centres, as well as a motivation to get 'bums on seats' to help demonstrate their need for continued funding.

The Corston Report (2007) was a key moment for (re)imagining women's experiences of the CJS and the need for gender-specific reform. Although much has been critiqued since the report's publication (see Women in Prison, 2017 for further information), it represents a watershed moment in feminist criminological campaigning for alternatives to women's imprisonment. Women's centres existed before Corston yet it was only after the report that their role as authentic alternatives to prison was legitimised. In short, the decades of feminist campaigning and international feminist scholarship was brought mainstream by Corston's interception. Women's centres' clientele consists of women who go there freely, non-statutory, and those who are ordered to go there by the court, statutory. As such, a centre performs conflicting roles: on the one hand, it is there to support women by offering domestic violence (DV) support, education courses, free food, sanitary products, counselling and free legal advice, and, on the other hand, it is there to punish women. This paradox cannot be ignored; for women who go there on a statutory basis experience many of the 'pains of imprisonment' (Sykes, 1958) simply displaced on to this alternative site.

This chapter will draw from existing literature and my own observations and auto/biographical reflections of working at one women's centre in the north-west of England, UK. I will refer to the women's centre by using the pseudonym River Centre (RC). I will interrogate the complexities of a space occupying multiple conflicting roles in women's lives, and expand upon the need for radical trauma-informed gendered care. Gender-responsive practice is frequently criticised for failing to recognise the heterogeneity of women (Shaw and Hannah-Moffat, 2000; Moore and Scraton, 2014). Women who entered RC either as voluntary service users or by court order did not have their heterogeneity acknowledged. There was no accounting for individual preferences or opportunities to state what services or treatment they would prefer. It is important to emphasise here that this is one researcher's experience of one women's centre, with a narrative that sits in opposition to the claims that women's centres inherently empower women (WBG, 2020). The practice observed at RC consolidates the oppression of women who are already marginalised and struggling to make assertive decisions. Likewise, HMI Probation (2020) notes that there is insufficient understanding of individuals' personal situations and diversity planning in some women's centres.

While it is important to note the good work of many women's centres, and the strong role that such centres play in women's desistance, it is also crucial that harms experienced in such centres are acknowledged. It is also paramount to problematise this neoliberal system that understands 'choice' on an individual level and this chapter intends to contribute to this critical examination and discussion. First, the chapter briefly presents the auto/biographical methodology, before discussing three themes found from my work at RC. The chapter concludes by returning to the question of whether women's centres are focused on empowerment or punishment and invites the reader to reflect on these related issues.

Methodology

This study is an auto/biographical discussion of the phenomena of women's centres. Data collection took place as an independent scholar while on a break from academia. As such, no direct quotes will be used from participants, and instead, I utilise the methodology of auto/biography that I have committed to in other publications (Ahearne, 2015; Ahearne, 2021). As I argued elsewhere, feminist epistemologies place value on disrupting dominant ways of knowing (Ahearne, 2021) and there is much to be gained from reflexive practice (Dragomir, 2020; Harding, 2020a; Pearce; 2020; Baldwin 2021; Keene, 2021). It is important that critical feminist criminological work challenges dominant understandings of the CJS and recognises women's centres as liminal and conflicted spaces.

It is important for this chapter to be understood in terms of personal experience and conceptualised through a critical feminist lens. My ethical considerations have been underpinned by 20 years of working with 'vulnerable' women (Ahearne, 2015; Ahearne, 2017) and a deep commitment to feminist theory and praxis. The chapter must be recognised as my account of one anonymous women's centre, although the findings can be transferable to a broader debate on the role of women's centres. Three main themes emerged in my work: 1) Spaces of surveillance and (re) traumatisation; 2) Responsibilisation agenda and being their 'sisters' keeper'; and 3) The erasure of vulnerability and 'undeserving victims'. These will be explored next.

Space of surveillance and (re)traumatisation

RC reports in public communications that it receives over 600 visitors a week. In reality, many of these figures relate to women who are repeat visitors; they are the same women who often attend every day of the week. The women signed in through an electronic log in at the reception of the centre after accessing RC through an intercom door. The women's centre is in a building that once housed a school, which adds to the backdrop of infantilisation and control typical of surveillance techniques observed in the punishment of women (see Carlen, 1983). The main space consists of a large community room with an attached kitchen; this space is open and there are no quiet corners to hide away and discuss matters privately, adding to a culture of surveillance. The women met with their Empowerment Advisers (EAs) in full view of everybody else, where anybody could hear their private conversations. The centre is known for its ability to provide support relating to DV and women are signposted through GP surgeries, the council, police and frequent networking events in the community. It is very much seen as a 'one-stop shop' where women can get benefit and housing advice, see a solicitor for free, access counselling and receive support for their status as victims. The very nature of the centre's funding relies on footfall, and therefore they need 'bums on seats' (Harding, 2020a; 2020b; Elfleet, 2021). Therefore, friendships that met outside this centre were discouraged by the EAs who hovered around the community room, effectively keeping the women under constant surveillance. The women were also discouraged from exchanging phone numbers and forging friendships that expanded outside of the centre. It is important to note that this is not standard practice across all women's centres.

Understanding that where women have experienced DV, family abuse and other forms of coercive control and sexual violence, the need to reclaim space is strong. Antonsdittir (2020) asserts that victim survivors of rape reclaim space in a temporary manner when rapists are incarcerated, and

I would argue that we need to (re)imagine the potentials for women's centres in terms of a reclaiming of space by women who have been marginalised and socially excluded. Deterring women from making friends that they see outside of the centre mirrored the coercive and controlling tactics of abusive and controlling relationships. For women's centres to be radical spaces of change, they need to identify these triggers and remedy them. Instead, Elfleet argues that women's centres could be considered as an extension of transcarceral surveillance and control of the most marginalised women in society (Elfleet, 2021).

The privatisation of the probation service in England and Wales in 2014[1] meant that many Community Rehabilitation Companies (CRCs) would not fund one-on-one casework with women, and instead, women were subjected to group activities (Howard League for Penal Reform, 2016). Women service users tend to respond well to one-on-one sessions as they can build personal trusting relationships and not have to reveal distressing experiences in front of strangers (Howard League for Penal Reform, 2016). At RC group work was prevalent. Likewise, women who were statutory service users were required to attend probation appointments that complete an amount of 'RARS' (Rehabilitation Action Requirements). RARs were introduced by the Offender Rehabilitation Act 2014 (HM Inspectorate, 2017).

The monthly timetable has an 'R' in the boxes of the activities that can count towards this requirement; however, offender managers who oversee the statutory service users also have the authority to use their discretion. For instance, counselling sessions may count towards this requirement, in addition to courses on substance addiction and DV. In some women's centres many of these services are provided by partnership organisations, but many, as with RC, are also run by in-house staff with little or no teaching or professional qualifications. This is extremely problematic and where this happens, there is no quality assurance for the teaching or trauma-informed pedagogical practice. The unstable funding and overstretched resources of some women's centres make it challenging to recruit highly qualified staff or to pay for specialist training – all of which impacts on the quality, consistency and permanency of services the women receive. Likewise, WBG (2020, p 21) acknowledges that the nature of this short-term and unstable funding for women's centres means that 'staff with specialist skills must be placed on notice of redundancy' (a legal requirement of funding remains unconfirmed and it is foreseeable that they might lose their jobs). This leads to a revolving door of unqualified staff on short-term contracts and reduces the desirability of skilled staff to apply for such roles.

In RC the 'in-house' courses on DV are designed and facilitated by unqualified staff, and while the facilitators are friendly and well meaning, the triggering nature of the material and the lack of psychological training and safeguarding means that vulnerable women can be harmed by such courses. There is also potential harm to employees who are facilitating these courses without professional supervision and frameworks and who are often survivors of domestic abuse themselves. There is a distinct lack of understanding of trauma (Harding, 2020a; 2020b) and instead women are encouraged to think positively and focus on their 'choices'. This neoliberal self-responsibilisation rhetoric (Hudson, 1997) does not acknowledge the deep and fractured nature of a history of sexual and DV. Women were encouraged to be herded into groups rather than seek one-to-one support from an EA. I felt this was inappropriate for women suffering from multiple mental health illnesses and traumas, and instead underpinned a 'tick-box' culture whereby funding is granted on footfall and statistics.

The DV courses at RC are designed and delivered by a staff member who asserts that she herself was a victim of domestic abuse. This (re)emphasises a choice rhetoric and an 'I can do it, and so can you' narrative that does not address the complex and structural restraints that keep women in abusive relationships. Nor does it account for coercive control and the multiple traumas that women experience throughout their lifetime. The centre operates within a paternalistic framework, and it is unclear what courses would benefit a professional woman who would dismiss a class making glitter wish jars or other unaccredited courses. HMI Probation argues that there can be insufficient understanding of DV and safeguarding risks in service delivery (HMI Probation, 2020) and, in my opinion, this applies to RC.

In my experience, I saw women being discouraged from talking about their trauma or distress in any setting other than counselling and related courses. The way in which trauma is managed is interrogated by the work of Harding (2021). Even in the case of the courses, there was a mould that the women were expected to fit into. It is all part of the 'happy' facade of the centre that everything should be light and cheery wherever possible. Harding refers to this as the 'management of trauma' (Harding, 2021). Women are not always given the opportunity to develop assertive thinking skills and the ability to locate and name their own trauma (Ahrens, 2006; Dragomir, 2020; Ahearne, 2021). Nor are they allowed to speak negatively about the CJS or the social inequalities that are also a source of violence to them. A noticeable example here is the lack of a complaints procedure against staff. This could represent a clear power dynamic issue as opposed to being 'accepted' that women service users were happy and content with the provisions of the RC. Harding (2020a) argues that women attending a women's centre undertaking community punishment are not afforded 'free time' to reflect, discuss and be heard in the way that healing from trauma allows. At RC this was an experience also shared by non-statutory women. Serious faces and low moods were dismissed with phrases like 'come on, put a smile on', and even a woman trying to have a quiet ten minutes alone with a cup of tea would find her attempts at solace punctuated with the roars of faux laughter from an EA and invitations to 'do' something. RC encouraged the women to constantly be in motion, even if that meant signing up to the same unaccredited course four or five times. In this way women were kept busy but not with meaningful activity that can address root issues. As such, it can be seen as a performance of punishment–lite, and has a 'warehouse function' towards women which leaves their needs unmet (Greenwood, 2019).

Responsibilisation agenda and being their 'sisters' keeper'

The privatisation of probation services and the increasing competition for funding has fuelled the neoliberal self-responsibilisation agenda (Concoran et al, 2020a; Elfleet, 2021). The dominant narrative is that women must make the 'choice' to change (Ahearne, 2016; Harding, 2020a; Elfleet, 2021; Harding, 2021). Viewing criminalised women's circumstances through the lens of choice removes the harms and traumas that most have endured. It legitimises dealing with women through the CJS and via an enforcement framework. Many women's centres are subject to 'gagging orders' imposed on them as conditions of their contracts with the Ministry of Justice. Therefore, due to the nature of much of the centre's funding, RC are not permitted to actively and outwardly show criticism of the government or the punitive welfare regime, including the rolling out of Universal Credit.[2] This is another example of the structural barriers women face and the poverty they endure as a result of being ignored. For example, RC had planned to have a speaker from the Department of Work and Pensions (DWP) as opposed to a speaker from charities who would criticise the welfare reforms. This served to silence and hide women's suffering and not give the women the opportunity to be critically minded and push back at the state, or to critically address the barriers to desistance.

Garland (1996) describes responsibilisation strategies as the central government acting upon crime in a non-direct fashion through state agencies, but instead acting indirectly, seeking to activate action on behalf of non-state agencies and organisations. Hannah–Moffat (2000, p 514) suggests that while the use of other agencies and volunteers in the role of punishment is not new, the relationship between the state and those agencies have changed as these new partnerships allow the government to govern 'at a distance'. The dismissal of the women's individual experiences at the RC and the lack of empathy can be framed and understood in this way. A feminist criminological perspective must be utilised in order to critique all of those services that do not seek to reform and challenge the patriarchal lens through which we judge women's reformation, else we merely replicate it in other sites. Given that these 'one-stop shops' hold access to a variety of help from legal advice, housing help, police drop-ins and substance support groups, it stands to reason that some women might feel cajoled into attending in order to access the service(s) they require, or are told they require. Control is exerted under the guise of 'protection' and monetary funds awarded to community-based interventions that women are required to attend (Ahearne, 2017). Kendal argues that 'the government's vision will ultimately result in growing numbers of people competing to participate in the punishment and control of women [and men] in prison and the community – in essence, to be their sisters' keepers' (Kendal, cited in Carlton and Segrave, 2013, p 43).

While non-custodial sentencing is a positive step, the fear is that structural factors that inform women's experiences with crime will go ignored (Clarke and Chadwick, 2019). This is something that I experienced throughout RC and is something that other researchers concur with (Greenwood, 2019; Harding, 2020a; Elfleet, 2021). It is important to not see a non-custodial sentence for women as an 'easier option'; Corston herself admits that community sentencing is not a soft-touch approach and women often find it harder than a custodial sentence (Corston, 2007). The women undertaking their community hours at RC do so under the Community Payback scheme, which the CEO of RC presented as a 'punitive approach'. The specific problem for women who undergo Community Payback and/or complete their RARS through the courses available at RC is that should they wish to continue gaining support, they cannot untangle themselves from the space of their punishment. In this way women may never physically or symbolically leave the site of punishment. The public sight of women performing menial labour in bright orange tabards is a public performance of incarceration and punishment, and revenge, and it acts as a spectacle to warn others of how to behave. The tabards worn by the women at the RC also created a form of social isolation and labelling, even when the women were on breaks inside the communal areas, with staff and other centre users avoiding those wearing the item. This process and practice of stigmatisation and effective shaming should be ceased. The tabards are humiliating and demeaning, and added to the women's sense of anxiety, shame and displacement (Greenwood, 2019; Harding, 2020a; 2020b). Interestingly, while at RC I was told by an EA that I was too 'smiley' with the women who perform tasks such as cleaning toilets, windows and garden work outside, which in my view illustrated the 'othering' of women who were seen primarily as 'criminals'. This aspect of punishment also highlights and brings into question the suitability of such centres for non-statutory women, many of whom have serious health problems.

Having to complete unpaid work via a 'one size fits all' approach also presents additional problems for mothers. If, for example, a child was sick and required its mother's care, or if mothers had issues with childcare cancellations, then the women may not be able to complete their hours.

In these circumstances the RC failed to recognise or accept these barriers, and the neoliberal framework of self-responsibilisation and subsequent punishment was reinforced. In effect, women were forced to choose between being a 'good' mother and being a 'good' offender. For women with anxiety and other mental health problems, knowing they would get such a blunt, inflexible response was not helpful. Mothers phoning to apologise that they could not attend due to child sickness were often dismissed as 'having excuses', revealing disconnect between the reality of lack of childcare and the barriers women face in keeping appointments. Similarly, on a broader scale, some criminalised women cannot afford to pay for childcare and therefore find it impossible to complete their hours. It cannot be a successful regime that forces mothers to choose between caring for their sick child or picking up litter for eight hours. Here again, in the RC this dilemma was reduced to a simplistic understanding of 'choice' for not coming in and completing their allocated hours. This fixation on women completing their hours has also been criticised by HMI Probation (2020), who stated that in the women's centre the primary focus on the completion of unpaid work was sometimes at the cost of the work to not reoffend. This then leads to the RARS days not being able to be completed, and implications for women breaching their court orders (HMI Probation, 2020). This demonstrates the lack of critical thinking at the expense of bureaucracy and a tick-box culture that seeks to obtain funding.

This dismissive neoliberal understanding of 'choice' is recognised in Harding's study (2020a; 2020b; see also 2021), and by Clarke and Chadwick (2019). This simplistic understanding of choice that is free from external constraints and structural inequalities is part of the neoliberal regime. Kendall argues that the increased involvement of the voluntary sector within the CJS in community-based programmes has 'entangled non-government and government agents in a hybridized widening net of governance' (Kendall, 2013, cited in Carlton and Segrave, 2013, p 45). We must critique and consider the complicated regimes of regulation, and how the government increasingly operates at a distance using other actors to exert forms of surveillance and control. This is not to deny that some women may personally benefit from women's centres, but to emphasise that women's centres can also represent an expansion and net widening of penal practices and infrastructure (Carlton and Segrave, 2013; Ahearne, 2017).

While RC cannot criminalise non-statutory women who attend, the failure to address structural marginalisation increases women's dependence on the centre for social support (Greenwood, 2019) and the precarious funding of the service forces it to rely upon the continued engagement of clients (Elfleet, 2021). It could therefore be argued that the centre effectively becomes a site of encouraged containment for vulnerable women. RC can then be understood as being a holding pen for women; this can be read through the livestock language of herding the women around into various holding pens such as the community room or the fitness hall. Women 'lulling about the place' are not bums on seats, and will not guarantee funding against the alleged successes of the courses. All women who attend are under the penal gaze and their behaviour is monitored and regulated. A participant in Greenwood's (2019) study emphasised this, indicating how staff wanted the women engaged in courses constantly. The focus then becomes not one of meaningful change or for courses that provide genuine benefit, but rather a series of tick-box exercises. This herding of women was repeated in Elfleet's study, where a worker states "they can't just come in here and not do anything, because that's not the point of the centre" (Elfleet, 2021, p 12).

The erasure of vulnerability and 'undeserving victims'

Women in the CJS occupy a liminal space by being presented as deviant, yet also as vulnerable. They are also presented as being uniquely vulnerable yet simultaneously have their vulnerability erased upon their entry to the CJS (Ahearne, 2016; 2019). Drawing from the work of Brown (2017), this vulnerability framework can be applied to the women who attended RC both in a voluntary and a court-ordered capacity. In the case of centres such as RC, women also have their trauma ignored due to the self-responsibilisation agenda (Elfleet, 2021) because it is seen as 'their choice' to make desired changes. While much of this simplistic dismissal of trauma is instigated by the funding model (Greenwood, 2019), it also speaks to the White, middle-class, feminist agenda that dominates women's 'reform' practices and in turn underpins gender-responsive reform (Hannah-Moffat and Shaw, 2000; Corston, 2007). One of the slogans of RC is the tagline 'Empowering women'. While the notion of 'empowerment' is much contested and has become a cheap buzzword for neoliberal, gender-responsive strategies, it is clear to me from my experience that the concept of 'empowerment' needs revisiting. Elfleet (2021) also argues that understandings of 'empowerment' have become divorced from their feminist origins. In Greenwood's study the women completing unpaid work as part of their community orders were asked if they felt empowered, and all participants answered that they did *not* feel empowered. Examples included pregnant women being made to complete their unpaid work in the pouring rain, and one participant asserting that the unpaid work was "slave labour" (Greenwood, 2019, p 222). We need to understand women inside the CJS as being vulnerable, and ensure that they can disclose when they are being harmed. Elfleet (2021) argues that at the women's centre where she collected data, understandings of 'empowerment' were vague and self-perpetuating. Elfleet also states that perceptions of empowerment at the women's centre were detached from recognition of structural inequalities. This reconciles with my experiences and understanding of RC and provides evidence for the importance of women with lived experience to have a role in the shaping of criminal justice responses (Booth and Harriott, 2021).

The ethos of a women's centre should be trauma-informed, and this is arguably paradoxical when people are being punished in the spaces said to be able to 'empower' them (Harding, 2020a). The Prison Reform Trust (2017, p 7) report that '79 per cent' of women accessing services with Women in Prison 'have reported experiencing DV or sexual abuse'. Lived experience of trauma and gendered violence is an important tool (Ahrens, 2006; Antonsdottir, 2020; Ahearne, 2021; Dragomir, 2020) for understanding the long-lasting consequences of experiencing such violations. McGlynn and Westmarland (2019) argue for the use of the term 'victim survivor' to best capture the varied experiences and identities of women who have been subjected to sexual violence. These authors also explore 'kaleidoscopic justice', which is a pluralistic conception of the different ways in which justice might be imagined by different actors. I argue that this terminology and these interrogations of justice are relevant here, with women able to label and understand their journeys and what services should look like. Given the frequency with which women experience sexual violence (Antonsdottir, 2020), women's centres must position women as victim survivors and build services around that. This can be understood in terms of my earlier argument regarding the lack of heterogeneity of services provided.

During Harding's landmark study she shared photo maps drawn by participants, including a woman called Nat (Harding, 2020a; 2020b). Nat's image shows a binary understanding of the 'good path' that she 'chose' to take as opposed to the 'bad' path she could have gone down, perhaps demonstrating the internalisation of 'good' and 'bad' choices that criminalised women feel (or are made to feel). Elfeet (2018) also emphasises this issue with a neoliberal governance strategy that places the burden of 'change' on to the individual woman while simultaneously obscuring the role of the state. As Harding rightly argues, the image stresses the importance of choice, 'flattening the distinct and layered oppression and social inequality experienced by criminalised women' (Harding, 2020b, p 10). Harding also argued that, as such, Nat was not seeing that the women are victims of trauma, and she certainly was not seeing criminalisation as a site of trauma. At the RC, senior empowerment workers oversaw the work of the EAs underneath them, and they worked directly in contact with the probation team who were housed in the same building. They ensured that the Community Payback hours were completed, by standing over the women as they weeded the communal garden, and they drove the van when the women were taken out to public spaces to paint fences. Staff at the centre utilised a simplistic ideology of women undertaking unpaid work as 'offenders' and not as traumatised women who could be (re)traumatised by the CJS (Harding, 2020b) via this public shaming in the pursuit of justice. This is a key issue and must be factored into the discussions of those who are pushing non-custodial options. An alternative site to prison that causes secondary and institutional trauma is problematic (Smith and Freyd, 2013; 2014). Greenwood's (2019) study demonstrates how women undertaking unpaid work in a women's centre experience their labour as embarrassing and a source of shame. Women also had fear and significant anxiety that they would be seen undertaking their court-ordered work by members of their family or community (Greenwood, 2019). Yet none of what has been mentioned here has been addressed by RC as problematic or something that the women need protecting from.

Understandings of victimhood have long been contested (Christie, 1986; Ahearne, 2021). Gilchrist (2010) argues that the news media perpetuate a hierarchy of female victims, whereby binary categories are often used to differentiate 'good' women from 'bad' women (see also Jewkes, 2004), and this is especially true of women who are also mothers (Baldwin, 2015; Booth, 2020; Masson, 2019). The women presented as being unworthy victims are often portrayed as being 'beyond redemption' and being undeserving of empathy (Jiwani, 2008). This is a double-edged sword for women undergoing court orders at RC who are both understood through this general lens as being unworthy victims, but also might have been in the local or national press for their criminal offence and thus have their individual stigma intensified. McEvoy and McConnachie (2012) problematise the need for 'innocence' for an actor to achieve victimhood status. This is important as people occupy multiple identities (Carlton and Segrave, 2013; Coomber, 2015; Ahearne, 2016; Ahearne, 2017) and it is possible for women to be offenders *and* victims (McEvoy and McConnachie, 2012; Ahearne, 2019). Therefore, it is crucial for centres such as RC to acknowledge the heterogeneity of women using the centre, and recognise how harmful it is for women to be 'helped' in the same space that they are punished.

Conclusion

It is clear that women should not be punished and helped in the same place. Women's centres which double up as sites where unpaid work takes place are replicating the harms of custodial settings and are not addressing the co-dependent relationships of former abuse and coercion. There must be adequate safeguarding underpinning all services and money must be invested in qualified staff and devising a trauma-informed strategy. The push for alternatives to women's imprisonment has meant a lack of critique of the harms of alternatives. I recommend an independent review into all women's centres that utilise unpaid work, and furthermore that any such review must at least include, but arguably be led by, women with lived experience of the CJS. It is of concern that women are being (re)traumatised in the spaces designed to help them with no recourse against the system that is causing them harm. The ongoing competition for funding for women's centres must be acknowledged as women competing to be their sisters' keeper, and as such, is opposed to genuine principles of empowerment and gender-responsive reform. Women must be at the centre of decisions made about them in order to develop positive strategies of desistance and connections to their communities.

The erasure of women's vulnerability when entering the CJS must be addressed, as must the construction of deserving and undeserving women. The discretion afforded to individual workers when supervising RARS must be implemented (HMI Probation, 2017) and an individualised strategy devised to ensure that women are not 'piled high' as part of a tick-box funding exercise. In doing so, women's needs as victim survivors of sexual and/or DV could be identified and a participatory–action relationship devised whereby women are given the opportunity to shape some of their RARS journey. There must be adequate safeguarding measures in place in order that women are able to report harms that occur during their unpaid work and completion of RARS. Barriers to completing unpaid work hours such as an inability to access childcare must also be addressed, so that criminalised mothers/carers are not penalised.

The role of women's centres that are sites of unpaid work orders can be understood as spaces of institutional warehousing (Greenwood, 2019; Harding, 2021) and must be analysed accordingly. Both prison abolitionists *and* those pushing for reform must acknowledge the violence of neoliberal gender-response forms that fail to name the state's failings. Instead, such understandings push a neoliberal feminist governance strategy that individualises the issue of women's offending without identifying the socio-economic deprivation and barriers in women's lives. A failure to address what has been mentioned here is being complicit with the feminisation of poverty and the structural brutality that women face. Painting women's centres pink will not be enough to overcome this; we have to ask, are women's centres spaces of empowerment or punishment?

Reflection points

- Why is it important to consider the potential of harm in spaces that operate as an alternative to imprisonment?
- Is it a paradox to suggest that women can be helped and punished in the same space?
- Why must structural inequalities be addressed when considering women's involvement with the CJS?

Acknowledgements

I would like to thank Dr Kirsty Greenwood for her comments on an earlier version of this chapter.

Notes

[1] This privatisation took place following the Transforming Rehabilitation agenda (2014) in England and Wales where probation services that were delivered by 35 Probation Trusts were divided, the high-risk offenders being the responsibility of a newly created National Probation Service, while CRCs were contracted to deliver interventions to low- and medium-risk offenders. However, in 2021 a further restructuring of probation services in England and Wales was announced with a considerable shift back to the previous National Probation Service.

[2] Universal Credit was introduced in 2013 and combined a number of existing benefits into one single payment for low-income and out-of-work persons. It has been criticised for a number of reasons – see House of Lords Economic Affairs Committee (2020) for more information.

References

Ahearne, G. (2015) Between the sex industry and academia: navigating stigma and disgust, *Graduate Journal of Social Science*, 11, 28–37.

Ahearne, G. (2016) Paying the price: sex workers in prison and the reality of stigma, *Prison Services Journal*, 223, 24–30.

Ahearne, G. (2017) *A Thematic Analysis of the Experiences of Women Sex Workers in Prison*, Unpublished PhD thesis, Leeds: Leeds Beckett University.

Ahearne, G. (2019) 'They only care when there's a murder on': contested perceptions of vulnerability from sex workers in prison, *British Journal of Community Justice*, 15(1) 67–76.

Ahearne, G. (2021) Criminologist or criminal? Liminal spaces as the site for auto/biography, *Methodological Innovations*, 14(1), https://journals.sagepub.com/doi/full/10.1177/20597991211012054.

Ahrens, C.E. (2006) Being silenced: the impact of negative social reactions on the disclosure of rape, *American Journal of Community Psychology*, 38, 263–74.

Antonsdottir, H.F. (2020) Injustice disrupted: experiences of just spaces by victim-survivors of sexual violence, *Social & Legal Studies*, 29(5), 718–44, doi:10.1177/0964663919896065.

Baldwin, L. (2015) *Mothering Justice: Working with Mothers in Criminal and Social Justice Settings*, Hampshire: Waterside Press.

Baldwin, L. (2018) Motherhood disrupted: reflections of post-prison mothers in maternal geographies, *Emotion Space and Society*, 26, 49–56.

Baldwin, L. (2021) Presence, voice and reflexivity in feminist and creative research: a personal and professional reflection, in Masson, I., Baldwin, L. and Booth, N. (eds.), *Critical Reflections from the Women, Families, Crime and Justice Research Network*, Bristol: Policy Press.

Booth, M. and Harriott, P. (2021) Service users being used: thoughts to the research community, in Masson, I., Baldwin, L. and Booth, N (eds.), *Critical Reflections on Women, Family, Crime and Justice*, Bristol: Policy Press, pp 199–218.

Brown, K. (2017) The governance of vulnerability: regulation, support and social divisions in action, *International Journal of Sociology and Social Policy*, 37(11–12), 667–82.

Carlen, P. (1983) *Women's Imprisonment: A Study in Social Control*, Abingdon: Routledge.

Carlton, B. and Segrave, M. (eds.) (2013) A radical vision for system social change, in *Women Exiting Prison: Critical Essays on Gender, Post-Release Support and Survival*, London: Routledge, pp 200–8.

Christie, N. (1986) The ideal victim, in Fattah, E. (ed.) *From Crime Policy to Victim Policy*, London: Palgrave Macmillan, pp 17–30.

Clarke, B. and Chadwick, K. (2019) From 'troubled' women to failing institutions: the necessary narrative shift for the decarceration of women post-Corston, in Moore, L., Scratton, P., and Wahidin, A., (eds.) *Women's Imprisonment and the Case for Abolition: Critical Reflections on Corston Ten Years On*, Abingdon: Routledge, pp 51–71.

Coomber, R. (2015) A tale of two cities: understanding differences in levels of heroin/crack market-related violence – a two city comparison, *Criminal Justice Review*, 40, 7–31.

Corston, J. (2007) *The Corston Report: A Review of Women with Particular Vulnerabilities in the Criminal Justice System*, London: Home Office.

Dragomir, C.-I. (2020) *Methodological Innovations*, 13(3), September, https://journals.sagepub.com/doi/full/10.1177/2059799120968728

Elfleet, H. (2018) Women's centres: gender responsive services for formerly imprisoned women post Corston Report 2007, *ECAN Bulletin*, 35, 17–22. Available from: https://howardleague.org/wp-content/uploads/2018/04/ECAN-bulletin-April-2018.pdf [Accessed: 16 February 2023].

Elfleet, H. (2021) Neoliberal feminised governmentality: the role and function of a post Corston Report (2007) women's centre in the north-west of England, *British Journal of Community Justice*, 16(2), 1–22. Available from: https://mmuperu.co.uk/bjcj/wp-content/uploads/sites/2/2021/04/Elfleet-H-Neoliberal-Feminised-Governmentality-Final-Copy.22.02.21.pdf [Accessed: 16 February 2023].

Garland, D. (1996) The limits of the sovereign state: strategies of crime control in contemporary society, *British Journal of Criminology*, 36, 445–71.

Gilchrist, K. (2010) 'Newsworthy' Victims? Feminist *Media Studies*, 10, 373–90, doi:10.1080/14680777.2010.514110.

Greenwood, K. (2019) *Statutory and Non-Statutory Service-Users' Experiences of Gender-Responsive Practice in a Post-Corston (2007) Women's Centre,* Unpublished PhD thesis, Liverpool: Liverpool John Moores University. Available from: www.theguardian.com/society/2020/jun/04/minist ers-considering-renationalising-england-and-wales-probation-service [Accessed: 20 June 2020].

Hannah-Moffat, K. and Shaw, M. (2000) *An Ideal Prison: Critical Essays on Women's Imprisonment in Canada,* Manitoba: Fernwood Books.

Harding, N.A. (2020a) *Navigating Gendered Criminalisation: Women's Experiences of Punishment in the Community,* Unpublished PhD thesis, Manchester: Manchester Metropolitan University.

Harding, N.A. (2020b) Co-constructing feminist research: ensuring meaningful participation while researching the experiences of criminalised women. Methodological Innovations, 13(2), https://doi.org/10.1177/ 2059799120925262.

Harding, N.A. (2021) Playing the game: women and community punishment, in *Critical Reflections on Women, Family, Crime and Justice,* Bristol: Bristol University Press.

HMI Probation (2017) The implementation and delivery of rehabilitation activity requirements, [online] February. Available from: www.justicein spectorates.gov.uk/hmiprobation/wp-content/uploads/sites/5/2017/ 02/Report-Rehabilitation-Activity-Requirement-Thematic-final.pdf [Accessed: 20 June 2020].

HMI Probation (2020) An inspection of probation services on Merseyside, [online] June. Available from: www.justiceinspectorates.gov.uk/hmiprobat ion/wp-content/uploads/sites/5/2020/06/Merseyside-CRC-v1.0.pdf [Accessed: 20 June 2020].

House of Lords Economic Affairs Committee (2020) Universal Credit isn't working: proposals for reform, [online] 31 July. Available from: https:// committees.parliament.uk/publications/2224/documents/20325/default/ [Accessed: 24 September 2021].

Howard League for Penal Reform (2016) Is it the end of women's centres?, [online]. Available from: https://howardleague.org/wp-content/uploads/ 2016/11/Is-it-the-end-of-womens-centres.pdf [Accessed: 21 June 2020].

Hudson, B. (1997) Social control, in Maguire, M., Morgan, R. and Reiner, R. (eds.) *The Oxford Handbook of Criminology* (2nd edn), Oxford: Oxford University Press.

Jewkes, Y. (2004) *Media and Crime,* London: Sage.

Jiwani, Y. (2008) Mediations of domination: gendered violence within and across borders, in Sarikakis, K. and Regan Shade, L. (eds.) *Feminist Intervention in International Communication: Minding the Gap,* Plymouth: Rowman & Littlefield, pp 129–45.

Keene, S. (2021) Becoming a sexademic: reflections on a 'dirty' research project, *Sexualities*, 25(5–6), 676–93, doi:10.1177/1363460720986915.

Masson, I. (2019) *Incarcerating Motherhood: The Enduring Harms of First Short Periods of Imprisonment on Mothers*, Abingdon: Routledge.

McEvoy, K. and McConnachie, K. (2012) Victimology in transitional justice: victimhood, innocence and hierarchy, *European Journal of Criminology*, 9(5), 527–38.

McGlynn, C. and Westmarland, N. (2019) Kaleidoscopic justice: sexual violence and victim-survivors' perceptions of justice, *Social & Legal Studies*, 28(2), 179–201, doi:10.1177/0964663918761200.

Moore, L. and Scraton, P. (2014) *The Incarceration of Women: Punishing Bodies, Breaking Spirits*, London: Palgrave Macmillan.

Pearce, R. (2020) A methodology for the marginalised: surviving oppression and traumatic fieldwork in the neoliberal academy, *Sociology*, 54(4), 806–24, https://journals.sagepub.com/doi/10.1177/0038038520904918.

Prison Reform Trust (2017) Majority of women in prison have been victims of domestic abuse, [online]. Available from: https://prisonreformtrust.org.uk/wp-content/uploads/old_files/Documents/Domestic_abuse_report_final_lo.pdf [Accessed: 10 November 2022].

Smith, C.P. and Freyd, J.J. (2013) Dangerous safe havens: institutional betrayal exacerbates sexual trauma, *Journal of Traumatic Stress*, 26, 119–24.

Smith, C.P. and Freyd, J.J. (2014) Institutional betrayal, *American Psychologist*, 69(6), 575–87.

Sykes, G. (1958) *The Society of Captives: A Study of a Maximum Security Prison*, Princeton: Princeton University Press.

Tavistock Institute Of Human Relations (2019) Why women's centres work: an evidence briefing, [online] May. Available from: www.tavinstitute.org/news/why-womens-centres-work-an-evidence-briefing/ [Accessed: 10 November 2022].

Terweil, A. (2020) What is carceral feminism?, *Political Theory*, 48, 421–42, doi:10.1177/0090591719889946.

Women's Budget Group (2020) *The Case for Sustainable Funding for Women's Centres: A Report from the UK Women's Budget Group*, London: WBG. Available from: https://wbg.org.uk/wp-content/uploads/2020/10/WBG-15-Womens-Centres-Report-v4.pdf [Accessed: 10 November 2022].

4

Silent victims: uncovering the realities of the criminal justice system for families of prisoners

Zobia Hadait, Somia R. Bibi and Razia Tariq Hadait

Introduction

This chapter explores women's and families' experiences of navigating the criminal justice system (CJS) once 'a loved one' (Masson and Booth, 2018) is arrested and imprisoned. We draw on our experiences as frontline community workers within Himaya Haven CIC[1] – a leading Birmingham-based organisation specialising in supporting families with someone in prison and/or custody. We explore and highlight the multi-layered and complex realities families of prisoners face. As discussed later, our support is accessible to all, but we find that most of our clients belong to groups situated within the category of Black and Minority Ethnic (BAME)[2] and are women. Therefore, this chapter draws attention to both cultural and gendered issues regarding *blame and stigma, financial difficulties* and *children and young people's experiences*. Academic scholarship and data from third and public sectors consistently illustrate how the social, domestic, financial, health and psychological hardships of families are often exacerbated by imprisonment (Murray and Farrington, 2005; Arditti et al, 2010; Dickie, 2013; Farmer, 2017). Not only does this place enormous pressure on loved ones supporting an imprisoned person, but it has ripple effects throughout society. Quoting Lord Farmer (2017), family bonds are 'the golden thread', playing a pivotal role in reducing and, to a degree, stopping reoffending and inter-generational crime. Supporting previous research (Codd, 2008; Masson and Booth, 2018), our frontline practitioner experiences have highlighted that who constitutes 'prisoners' families' is not clear cut, and not all family bonds are supportive and positive. Accordingly, we identify two types of prisoners' families requiring support:

- 'Those supporting a family member in prison and are struggling practically and emotionally' (Bibi, 2021, np);
- 'People who need the CJS to help shield themselves from [a] family member in prison' (Bibi, 2021, np).

Presently, 98 per cent of families who seek support from Himaya Haven are from the first category and so our services are often targeted towards this group (Bell, 2021). Our frontline work highlights the real issues that need to be considered at the intersection of race, culture, faith, gender and age when looking at prisoners' families. Such factors pose an experience of the CJS that is individual to each family member. Navigating the CJS can be a potentially new and unfamiliar process for families, with difficulties spanning from the point of arrest, through remand, imprisonment and after release (Sharp et al, 1997; Abass, 2015; Masson and Booth, 2022). Consequently, families need support through a multi-agency approach independent and impartial from the CJS.

When exploring the impact on prisoners' families, race plays a significant role in determining who constitutes this large proportion at a global and national level. Indeed, within England and Wales, BAME individuals constitute 40 per cent of those in youth custody and 25 per cent of the prison population, despite representing only 14 per cent of the general UK population (Lammy, 2017). This disproportionately reflects the continued existence of structural racism and inequality in both wider society and the CJS, which has been highlighted by several reviews (Lammy Review, 2017 and MacPherson Report, 1999). The high density of BAME prisoners is mirrored by Himaya Haven prisoners' families, most of whom are classified as BAME, largely coming from Pakistani and Kashmiri backgrounds (Bibi, 2020). This demographic is likely reflective of Birmingham's population, which is largely South Asian and Muslim. For instance, we have previously reported that Muslims constitute over a quarter (27 per cent) of the population in this area (see Bibi, 2020, p 32).

Our clients also come from economically disadvantaged communities in Birmingham, like Bordesley Green, Alum Rock, Saltley and Small Heath. We also have long-distance clients from Derby, Manchester and London, whom we provide regular telephone support. Research shows that British Pakistanis have the highest proportion of households living in poverty at 45 per cent (Barnard, 2014), with higher unemployment rates and concentrated in lower-paying occupations (Brynin and Longhi, 2015). Within this context, imprisonment of a family member can bring additional economic hardships as BAME loved ones must juggle these employment challenges alongside the costs associated with prison, like the reduction of household income alongside funding prison visits (Codd, 2008).

Furthermore, the larger number of male prisoners compared with female prisoners in the UK[3] (Ministry of Justice [MoJ], 2021) means there is a significant gender disparity in those seeking support to navigate the CJS. Between 1 April 2020 and 30 March 2021, 95 per cent of Himaya Haven cases (where the gender of the prisoner was recorded) related to imprisoned men or boys, which follows demographics of clientele supported in previous years (Bell, 2021). Echoing previous research with prisoners' families (Codd,

2008; Booth, 2020; Booth and Masson, 2021), we find the majority of our clients identify as female (Bibi, 2020). Most report being the prisoner's mother or wife/partner (79 per cent between 1 April 2020 and 30 March 2021), while the smaller number of male clients report being a father, brother or husband. Reflective of this clientele group, much of this chapter focuses on the experiences of BAME female family members supporting boys/men in prison. It is through working with women in the community that we encounter children and young people with a parent or sibling in prison. Much of the literature exploring children's experiences indicates several challenges associated with familial imprisonment (Jones et al, 2013; Robertson et al, 2016; Masson, 2019). Likewise, parental imprisonment is considered an adverse childhood experience (ACE).[4] An understanding of ACEs is imperative for anyone working with and on behalf of children with imprisoned parents. Though imprisonment of parents is an ACE category, the probability of such children experiencing further ACEs is very high (Turney, 2018; Kincaid et al, 2019). As there is less focus on the experiences of BAME prisoner families (Abass, 2015), this chapter draws attention to the experiences of children and young people we have supported at Himaya Haven.

Defining 'the silent victims'

Before discussing the work and insights from our practitioner roles at Himaya Haven, it is important to outline our perspective regarding the way in which loved ones of prisoners are – and should be – positioned and labelled. We believe that conceptualising prisoners' families as 'the silent victims' on the outside is vital to recognising their needs and providing support. Previous scholars and commentators have similarly positioned prisoners' families as 'forgotten victims' (Matthews, 1983), 'orphans of justice' (Shaw, 1992, p 41), and the 'hidden victims of imprisonment' (Cunningham and Baker, 2003, p 2). This positionality shines a light on the stark reality that prisoners' families are significantly impacted by the imprisonment of a family member. We argue that the label of 'silent victims' needs to be mainstreamed and utilised across sectors, governmental bodies and the media. Its symbolism is powerful and vital. Razia Tariq Hadait, CEO and Managing Director of Himaya Haven, explains: 'They're the silent victims on the outside because no one recognises them as being victims. People think they don't suffer, but they do suffer. They suffer in silence because they don't want to talk about having someone in prison' (Bibi, 2021, np).

Traditionally, victims are defined as 'someone or something that has been hurt, damaged or killed or has suffered, either because of the actions of someone or something else, or because of illness or chance' (Cambridge Dictionary, 2021). We can attach the word 'victim' to those who have a loved one in custody or prison from this definition. This is because suffering occurs for family members who have themselves not committed any harm, but who experience disadvantages from the actions and situation of another person – their loved one. It is evident the families of those imprisoned or transitioning through the CJS can also experience trauma, isolation, stigma and abuse (Condry, 2007; Booth, 2020). Although they are not (always) on the receiving end of crime like traditional victims, they still face victimisation from society due to the crime(s) of their loved ones. Due to shame and embarrassment, many prisoners' families suffer in silence (Kotova, 2014). For BAME families, cultural shame and stigma can lead to further challenges (Abass, 2015; Ganeshpanchan and Masson, 2021). Identifying prisoner families as silent victims is something that should be acknowledged by society and professionals so that their needs and experiences are not ignored, and to ensure that families can be adequately and appropriately supported.

The ramifications of imprisonment for prisoners' families are potent. Comfort's (2009) work in the USA has maintained that prisoners' families are secondarily prisoned. She defines 'secondary prisonization' as 'a weakened but still compelling version of the elaborate regulations, concentrated surveillance, and corporeal confinement governing the lives of ensnared felons' (Comfort, 2009, p 2). Scholarship within the UK also reaffirms that imprisonment leads to an assortment of difficulties for prisoners' families (Smith et al, 2007; Farmer, 2017; Booth and Masson, 2021). Yet, families still do not garner the attention they need within the judicial system, and their struggles are also obscured within public discussions and narratives looking at the CJS; they have a 'disenfranchised social status' (Booth, 2020, p 17). We hope that by writing this chapter, and continuing our work at Himaya Haven, we can begin to make a difference to the lives and experiences of these silent victims.

Himaya Haven: our mission, services and clientele

Given the status of loved ones as 'silent victims', Himaya Haven's mission is to provide culturally sensitive services to meet their needs while they progress through the CJS. Himaya Haven was established as a grassroots, not-for-profit organisation in March 2017 in response to an identified need to support loved ones of people in contact with the CJS. The impetus for the organisation came from knowing an individual who experienced her son's remand into prison custody accused of a serious offence. Their struggles navigating the CJS accompanied by a lack of information and support following the separation prompted the decision to establish a community-based organisation to provide much-needed support and guidance.

Offering holistic support, advice, guidance, information, coping therapies and access to mainstream services (see Bibi, 2020), we find ourselves in an important position of trust by the silent victims on the outside.[5] Our services to this community include mentoring, advocacy, befriending, one-to-one support, prison/family information, court support, advice and guidance. We offer families home visits (where appropriate), outreach work, information and signposting. We aim to advocate for the silent victims by offering various services to support families of men and women who have a link with someone in custody or prison. We champion their needs and problems, assisting them to cope with the anxieties and practicalities of arrest, sentencing, imprisonment and release. We also tackle more taboo subjects which carry with them stigma, shame, and – more culturally associated – dishonour. These prominent and intersecting issues we experience as frontline practitioners are a likely reflection of the larger proportion of clients from BAME communities and their differing familial needs and circumstances (Mahmood and Mohammad, 2014; Hough, 2017). Understanding cultural and faith-related issues, and ensuring interventions are appropriately tailored, is an important facet of our work. As Hough (2017, p 163) states: 'specialist support can be crucial to a South Asian/ Muslim family in overcoming their own cultural and emotional difficulties over a family member's incarceration'.

Methods

As a community-based organisation, we try to collect some basic demographic information about our clients at Himaya Haven including name, age, ethnicity and relationship to the person in prison. This is recorded following GDPR guidelines and clients are informed that, after anonymisation, this information will be included in the public domain, such as annual reports (see Bibi, 2020) and funding bids. Likewise, some clients have given permission for their experiences to be discussed in other published works and so the client information and quotes shared in later sections of this chapter are being included, anonymously, with consent. This means that all names are pseudonyms and that any identifying information has been removed.

Working as the only community-based organisation in Birmingham providing a service for the silent victims of people in prison, we practitioners have a duty to unmask the lived consequences of families' experiences. The issues discussed in this chapter have been purposely selected to represent common experiences of clients supported by Himaya Haven. Three themes are to be discussed: 1) Blame and stigma, 2) Financial difficulties, and 3) Children and young people's experiences. As previously mentioned, at Himaya Haven we often work with female loved ones of prisoners, which echoes previous research and work with prisoners' families (Condry, 2007; Codd, 2008; Booth and Masson with Dakri, 2022). We also work primarily with BAME families and so we encourage the reader to consider the following three sections through a cultural and gendered lens.

Blame and stigma

Research shows that South Asian and Muslim prisoners can feel a great deal of shame when imprisoned (Arjoo, 2017; Ganeshpanchan and Masson, 2021). Mahmood and Mohammad's (2014) survey of South Asian/Muslim prisoners revealed that 75 per cent of respondents felt they had lost respect with their families due to their offending, and 36 per cent stated that specialist cultural and religious support would help them avoid trouble in the future. This shame expands beyond the criminalised individual and can be ascribed to, and experienced by, their loved ones in the community, a reality that requires careful recognition and tailored support. Additionally, arrest and imprisonment for (BAME) prisoners' families – particularly wives and mothers – causes feelings of isolation, discrimination, depression, shame, stigma, blame and dishonour and they are too embarrassed by their loved ones' actions to admit their arrest and/ or imprisonment. Similar findings have been reported in research with predominantly White family members of prisoners (see Condry, 2007; Codd, 2008; Kotova, 2014; Booth, 2020). To further illustrate how this can be experienced by our clientele, the following case study outlines Fozia's circumstances and experiences.

Case study 1: Fozia

Fozia, a 44-year-old British Pakistani client, with her 10-year-old son, was referred by the Children's Trust to Himaya Haven due to her husband being on a Sexual Harm Prevention Order for sexually assaulting a male under 13 (not their son). Fozia kept her husband's imprisonment a secret from all but her husband's immediate family for two years. For this reason, she concealed the fact she was on Jobseeker's Allowance;[6] when coming across family on the street returning or going to a Jobseekers appointment, Fozia would say she was visiting the doctor. Now a single mother, she is focused on successfully raising her son and developing the skills she needs to live an independent life, like taking classes to improve her written and oral English.

Himaya Haven were able to support the family by:

• Providing a safe space for Fozia to speak, share and reflect on her concerns, fears and hopes, which was provided via phone and face-to-face meetings;
• Conferring and corresponding with Fozia's husband's probation officer to clarify Fozia's legal rights and gain details on stipulation of licence conditions;

- Conferring with the probation officer to have the housing rental contract changed to Fozia's name;
- Researching when Fozia would need to apply for a Non-Molestation Order and informing her of this;
- Mentoring Fozia's son through the provision of educational support;
- Helping to locate a service to support with a British divorce and, with permission, completing the divorce application on her behalf;
- Locating information and processes of Islamic divorce and explaining this;
- Applying for court fee remittance on Fozia's behalf;
- Making referrals to relevant organisation(s) to help her with a housing application;
- Providing food hampers via our Christmas and Ramadan projects.

Fozia's experience is like many of our female clients who report that when members of the community and/or extended family find out about the imprisonment, they often begin to distance themselves from those affected, including the loved ones. Hence, prisoners' families are singled out, receiving very little or no emotional support, facing isolation and loneliness. What can make matters worse is when the prisoner has committed a crime (for example, a sexual offence), leading to local and/or national media coverage, making the person in prison visible to members of the community who may not have otherwise known. This increases the level of shame and embarrassment the family faces (Jones et al, 2013; Winder et al, 2020). This is no different to a low-profile case either, where fear of judgement may still exist, meaning that families may suffer from a lack of support. This is demonstrated by our client Annie, whose son was imprisoned: "Since this has happened I have not spoken to anyone. There is no support here. I don't know who to go to" (Annie).

Female partners and mothers of prisoners can also face rumours circulating in their local community about themselves, their imprisoned loved ones and their family. This, while also experiencing the traumatic loss associated with imprisonment on their own, can lead to anxiety, depression and in the worst cases paranoia. While facing judgement for actions which they are not responsible for heightens the likelihood of poor mental health. Commonly, across (BAME) prisoners' families, when a family member is imprisoned it is hidden from the wider community/family (Abass, 2015) by announcing upon questioning that the person in prison has gone 'back home' for a holiday, work or to build property, allowing them to avoid further questioning. Within our casework some family members may deny that a crime was committed, while also producing false stories of how their loved one happened to become a part of this crime. This can also be a result of shock and is the easiest way to 'ignore' the truth of the matter, becoming a useful defence mechanism while families get to grips with what has happened (Horowitz, 1986). This was experienced by Noreen when her son was arrested and imprisoned. Just the thought of explaining the imprisonment to her family, and the possible negative reactions that this might evoke, meant that she ignored a direct question via text about his incarceration, saying: "I tried to keep it from my family. Then the family were told … I have friends who've heard about my son being in prison. They've texted me. To this day I haven't replied because I don't know what to say to them" (Noreen).

When secrecy about the imprisonment has not been possible, we find that some wives/partners with no previous independence or confidence may feel obligated or pressured to 'stand by their man'. We witness some partners being pressured by their family and/or in-laws to stay with their partner, as a united front. They fear they will lose their security (for example, emotional/ financial support from immediate family, in-laws and husband upon release) and will be shunned by others if they do not comply. Additionally, many do not want to face the taboo title of being divorced – which unfortunately is still not widely accepted within South Asian/ethnic communities (Bibi, 2021; Singh, n.d.). Women who may not be knowledgeable or confident in communicating in English or able to make sense of the law may be coerced into staying so that they can keep their children as they do not know how to receive the support to challenge this.

Within South Asian households, cultural norms and expectations mean women are often blamed for the perceived failings of their children, as is the case across societies where women are positioned as naturally maternal and primary carers for children. In a similar way to the mothers of prisoners convicted of serious offences in Condry's (2007) study, this blame adds to already-existing stressors, compounding the emotional strain a mother experiences when her child is arrested and imprisoned. We have observed how blame is often internalised, and where it is not, female clients often feel they are being blamed. Consider the words of British Pakistani and single mother 56-year-old Alisha, whose 16-year-old son is involved in postcode gangs: "I don't know where I went wrong; I don't know what else I can do. He wants to be a gangster. He thinks of it like a job" (Alisha).

Culturally, we find when a child is doing 'well' the father is praised by society, yet when they are misbehaving and on the wrong path the mother is blamed, and at fault. Where a child has been imprisoned blame is also placed on the mother (Toor, 2009), particularly from the child's father. Within South Asian families, women's social status is likely to be dependent and influenced by the status of their male relative who is in prison. Unlike a male relative with a female family member imprisoned, the social stigma does not transfer in the same way. Men's social status is not usually dependent on their imprisoned female relative (Hannem, 2008). For women, their identities and how they are perceived are more likely to be impacted detrimentally by the imprisonment of their male relative. This amount of strain on individuals who may not be receiving the appropriate level of emotional and practical support is unimaginable. Consequently, the experiences of women from BAME prisoner families presented and discussed here, show how cultural norms and stigma create an environment of unease and shame for families. It is hoped that by sharing our practitioner insights that the reader can appreciate how they can easily end up suffering in silence, while still grieving for a close loved one.

Financial difficulties

Another pattern observed with clients supported by Himaya Haven is that when a male is imprisoned, the females – mostly partners/wives and mothers – must take on the traditionally 'male' role of the breadwinner. In traditional familial settings which still dominate within South Asian households, the father/husband occupies the role of the breadwinner (Ganeshpanchan and Masson, 2021). Even today where a woman may be working, the second male income is important and would be lost by imprisonment, putting a strain on the mother/wife. With most of our clients being from Pakistani/Kashmiri backgrounds, their culture upholds this traditional familial setting even if the mother/wife is earning her own income. As such, following imprisonment women must transition into the breadwinner role to ensure the financial stability of the household. Codd (2008) found that families can experience economic hardships when the breadwinner's income (whether via legal or illegal means) is removed following imprisonment. BAME women in this position face tremendous emotional and psychological shock and discomfort caused by many of them having never worked before and/or having been financially reliant on their families initially, followed by their partner/husband.

The resulting implication is that women must familiarise themselves with public transport routes, navigate the jobcentre process(es), create CVs, apply for jobs and apply for council housing. Yet, barriers include not knowing how to drive or how to pay bills (for example, rent, household/grocery bills and taxes). Some may not have the education/qualifications to undertake a job that allows them to balance their home and work life, some cannot find suitable employment while others must work very low-income jobs. In some cases, it is not until a person is imprisoned that unspoken debts are revealed. This is particularly hard for those we support at Himaya Haven because of cultural gendered roles meaning many women were not previously involved in financial affairs.

Due to this lack of understanding of policies and/or online processes, women are more likely to face financial sanctions. For instance, failing to attend a jobcentre appointment or apply online can result in much-needed benefits being stopped. As with Fozia's example, we find that many women may not have told their families about their child or spouse's imprisonment;

blocking any possible avenue of family support. Consequently, it is not uncommon for Himaya Haven practitioners to complete applications on clients' behalf and/or make referrals to other organisations who specialise in application processes. However, during the COVID-19 pandemic providing this support was a little more challenging. With most of our clients being Kashmiri and Pakistani with little English, we support them by translating key documents, finance/benefit letters and court letters. Our work translating to Urdu, Hindi and Punjabi helps alleviate emotional strain and ensures clients are in a better position to comprehend what can be quite complicated and contradictory information. Normally, clients would bring their letters in person; but, during the pandemic we had to translate these via WhatsApp.

We must be mindful that loved ones of prisoners are often from socially disadvantaged communities (Jardine, 2018) where digital illiteracy – as well as the aforementioned language barriers, access to internet data and devices – is not uncommon. With several services moving online and/or virtual during COVID-19, we observed how this pandemic has potently highlighted and exacerbated social, economic and health inequalities for the families we support. Language barriers – both before and during COVID-19 – also affect women getting aid because of a lack of understanding of what support is available, leaving them with no recourse to public funds. In such cases, inter-agency collaboration and communication is key to ensure such families are not left isolated and in severe economic hardship. Case study 2 outlines the financial circumstances of Taiyaba following her husband's imprisonment.

Case study 2: Taiyaba

Taiyaba, a returning Himaya Haven client in October 2020, remained actively engaged until April 2021 with a series of queries about benefits, finances and wider support for her and four children. Her husband has been imprisoned for over two years, and she has been struggling to learn and understand changes in her child benefit, policies such as those concerning council tax and how to manage her money. She does not speak English fluently so finds it difficult to understand information sent to her.

Himaya Haven were able to support the family by:

- Making a successful application to the COVID-19 Resilience Fund for the family;
- Supporting her husband's transfer to a prison closer to Taiyaba, enabling them increased visitation contact;
- Arranging for Taiyaba to attend ESOL and IT courses, increasing her independence;
- Reviewing her housing and council tax benefit entitlement and referring her to a specialist benefits charity;

- Supporting the family to apply for Free School Meal vouchers involving school correspondence;
- Aiding Taiyaba in investigating and disputing her water bills debt, saving her over £2,000;
- Applying for exemption from council tax for both children at university;
- Creating online accounts, including one with the local council;
- Assisting Taiyaba in successfully applying for Jobseeker's Allowance;
- Mentoring her two young children and helping them learn skills like communicating via letters and drawings with their father due to his illiteracy and how to use stamps and post letters;
- Providing food hampers via our Christmas and Ramadan projects and arranging weekly food bank deliveries.

Alongside these newly acquired financial responsibilities, women are also continuing to undertake tasks traditionally assigned to them. This can include, but is not limited to, taking the children to and from school, making meals, housework and fulfilling familial duties (looking after parents and/or in-laws). Given these domestic and caregiving responsibilities, women may only be able to work part-time and thus not have enough income to live as they once did. It is also the partners'/mothers' responsibility to provide the prisoner with funds to pay for their food, telephone costs, clothes, toiletries and TV licence, adding an incredible economic burden on to the families (Jardine, 2018; Booth, 2020). While earning and living on low income or benefits, the financial hardships that families – especially women – of prisoners face certainly change and intensify.

Children and young people's experiences

While working with women at Himaya Haven, we have also tailored services to support children and young people experiencing parental (often paternal) and sibling imprisonment. There are no formal data collection mechanisms to indicate the number of children affected by imprisonment annually in England and Wales, but most recent estimates indicate the figure could be as high as 310,000 (Kincaid et al, 2019). We recognise, from the literature (Masson, 2019) and our practitioner experience, that not all children will respond to having a parent in prison the same way; lived experiences are multidimensional and complex. Nevertheless, there are commonalities in what many children of prisoners will directly experience and face, including changes/deterioration in behaviour, anger, guilt, self-blame, shame, isolation (Jones et al, 2013; Robertson et al, 2016; Masson, 2019) and economic deprivation and disadvantage (Kincaid et al, 2019). Given what we have already learnt about the pressures facing BAME women with incarcerated loved one(s) in this chapter, it is perhaps unsurprising to learn how children and young people pick up on these emotions, stresses and pressures. Himaya Haven's client, Iram, reveals how the imprisonment of her brother while she was a child had – and continues to have – a significant impact on her, saying:

> 'My mother was devastated – it was like a funeral in the house. … Seeing your mother in this state has a profound and silent impact on a young child. The child cannot seek help as the child does not know the damage that is being done to him or her at the time, but it is long lasting and affects you in adulthood as it makes you paranoid about raising your own children.' (Iram)

Concerns in policy literature about inter-generational crime (Farmer, 2017) originate from older quantitative research (Murray and Farringdon, 2005) which reported correlations between parental offending and children's antisocial/criminal behaviour. Similarly, we see how Iram's concerns about her brother's incarceration while she was a child have created some anxieties about her own mothering experience. Some of this concern for inter-generational crime might come from worries about the social and financial disadvantage that BAME families experience in light of the imprisonment. Abass et al (2016) found that BAME children experiencing paternal imprisonment who are in their early teens and at a working age can feel obligated to help their mother out with the household bills. The financial strain(s) on a prisoner's family is significant and so when a child can comprehend the struggles that their parent is undergoing, they often take on family responsibilities. However, we have observed how this can sometimes be taken advantage of by gang leaders. Windle et al (2020) suggested that children of prisoners are exploited for their vulnerability and encouraged to join criminal gangs so that they can run drugs. Gangs take advantage of marginalised children and lure them in with money, gifts and a sense of security that they may not be accessing at home due to the hardship brought about by the imprisonment. This is likely appealing to children and young people who find it difficult to pay for new items (for example, clothing, footwear and iPhones) that other children of their age have (Robinson et al, 2019; Windle et al, 2020).

Furthermore, there have been concerns about children of prisoners 'falling through the cracks' for over a decade (Department for Children, Schools and Families (DCSF and MoJ, 2007), with schools being identified as an appropriate site to recognise and support vulnerable children (Jones, 2021). However, owing to fears of (cultural) stigma – for BAME families – many mothers may decide against disclosing the imprisonment to schools or other agencies. Children may also be encouraged to keep the whereabouts of the imprisoned loved ones a secret from peers and teachers (see Lockwood and Raikes, 2015). Previously mentioned engagement with the families we support reveals that there are cultural nuances in the experience of the loss of someone imprisoned. Within BAME families such as those from a Pakistani background, depending on the offence, the family of the prisoner can become ostracised by their extended family. It is also common within BAME families for other family and community members to visit the house when someone has been imprisoned to gather information about what has happened – but not always in a spiteful manner. We find that this does not give the chance for the family to grieve their recent and sudden loss, as they are too consumed in tending to their guests' needs and end up neglecting themselves and their children who are trying to process this new situation. Children can therefore close themselves up, as was the case for Sabrina's children who were experiencing the imprisonment of a sibling: "The incident has had a big impact on my other boys. They've become hard work for me. They need support; they won't talk to me. My youngest is 11. So many people have spoken to him about his brother being in prison. Like the word gets out" (Sabrina).

Despite the challenges facing BAME children and young people with a prisoner in the family, we contend that they remain the 'silent victims' whose experiences and struggles are widely overlooked and under-supported. Hames and Pedreira (2003, p 377) postulate that the reactions of children with imprisoned parents are reflective of reactions of children whose parents have died: 'too frequently these children, like children whose parents have died, are disenfranchised grievers coping with compounded losses'. Similarly, Raikes' (2014) research shows that feelings of 'ambiguous loss' are common among children of prisoners. Although parental imprisonment may benefit a small number of children, the majority are potently affected by the separation that is described as an experience 'akin to a bereavement' (Raikes, 2014, p 21). The following case study illustrates some of the impact parental imprisonment has on children.

Case study 3: Anika

Anika, at 12 years old, is the oldest of three children and has struggled exceptionally since her father was imprisoned. Anika's father will serve several years in prison. Since his arrest Anika has been clinging to her mother, exhibiting anger and anxiety, and refusing to go to school. Anika and her mother Rizwana were referred to Himaya Haven by Birmingham's Children's Trust. Rizwana found herself navigating new terrain when her husband was imprisoned. Unused to being the parent that enforces rules, she struggles to manage Anika's needs while implementing rules. Hence, Anika's attendance has significantly dropped, manipulating her anxiety to get her mother to concede to her wishes.

Anika had become resistant to engaging with the support work at school, as she felt they were not listening to her. We decided to step in due to Anika coming from a prisoner family and the fact her behaviour and actions presently put her wellbeing at risk. The impact of this was rippling through her family and causing emotional strain for all involved. Furthermore, Anika's emotional and mental health difficulties were exacerbated by the consequences of the COVID-19 pandemic on prison visits. During the lockdown prison visits were suspended, and while Anika received a daily phone call from her father, she struggled to adjust to the lack of face-to-face contact.

Himaya Haven stepped in to provide mentoring and support, including:

- Providing Anika with mechanisms to deal with anxiety;
- Creating a safe space for Anika to share and reflect on her thoughts and feelings;
- Communicating with the school to ensure multi-agency collaborative support was given to Anika and her family;
- Liaising with the school on behalf of Anika's mother;
- Encouraging Anika to attend school;
- Delivering educational support;
- Providing mother and daughter with meditation videos.

Yet children in prisoner families elicit far less sympathy in society (Masson, 2019) despite having committed no infractions themselves. Considering this context, we are motivated to continue working with children and young people and providing practical support (as outlined in the previous case studies), as well as emotional support, to this group.

Conclusion

Drawing on our frontline practitioner experiences while working with Himaya Haven, this chapter has revealed some of the specific challenges facing (mostly) women and children from BAME communities following the incarceration of a male relative. It is our contention that this group are 'silent victims' as our role exposes us, first-hand, to the many challenges loved ones of prisoners are faced with, and more often than not have to deal with alone. Every case we come across is individual, posing different issues and complexities; however, families of prisoners end up suffering the consequences of the crime too, while having nothing to do with it. We have highlighted the *blame and stigma* associated with incarceration and indicated how this may be more intense for women from BAME communities. This can lead to women isolating themselves and trying to cope alone with the difficult circumstances following imprisonment. We discussed the crippling *financial difficulties* and obligations partners and mothers of BAME prisoners are faced with, exacerbated by challenges of language barriers, low education (if any) and cultural pressures. Finally, we outlined BAME *children and young people's experiences* of parental and sibling imprisonment and, again, highlighted where cultural issues relating to gang and ostracism by extended family can shape their experiences. What our frontline work has shown is that families of prisoners are a marginalised group of society that is often forgotten, yet they need a lot of external support. At Himaya Haven, this is something we strive to do through our community-based service provision, but we also feel there are some changes that could be implemented, and these recommendations are highlighted here.

First, inter-agency collaboration is key. Currently, when a parent or sibling of a child is imprisoned, there is no contact between the judicial system and the schools. Having inter-agency support and communication in place is a crucial part of the families' coping and healing processes. We suggest that within schools, children, and parents (via workshops), are taught during Personal, Social, Health, Economics (PSHE) classes about imprisonment and the effect it leaves on the family and the various struggles they are faced with. Crime is often spoken about to children, but the long-lasting effects of imprisonment on the prisoner and family are not openly discussed in these settings. Having these discussions can facilitate acceptance of prisoner families and more importantly reduce the stigma and shame surrounding this. This will aid in positive mental health experiences pertaining prisoner families and provide them with the knowledge of appropriate support agencies out there who can provide expert advice and guidance where schools cannot.

Similarly, we contend that inter-agency collaboration, support and knowledge exchange is important between criminal justice and third-sector organisations. Presently, a key barrier to supporting prisoners' families is the lack of rigour when it comes to referrals from the police and courts. The red tape and administrative framework needed is not there, and with the existing responsibilities, the police face difficulties in managing an effective referral system. A review is thus needed at a national and local level, as is the cultivation of a referral pathway across sectors and agencies. Throughout this chapter we have aimed to highlight and discuss the specific challenges facing BAME families of prisoners, especially at the intersection of culture and gender. Our work has shown that women from BAME backgrounds often potently bear the burden on the outside when a loved one is imprisoned, often navigating new and unclear terrain without an awareness of the CJS and processes. Organisations such as Himaya Haven are there to provide support, yet currently, such organisations need to be more compellingly signposted by the governmental organisations and police.

Finally, due to the high number of BAME prisoners in the UK, more focus needs to be given to funding and providing culturally sensitive support via the third sector and undertaking practices that recognise the nuances and cultural norms that shape BAME families' lived experiences of having a loved one imprisoned. Criminal justice practitioners and policy matters going forward need to integrate into policy and frameworks of action, incorporating the experience and knowledge of frontline third-sector organisations and workers who support prisoner families. Moreover, prisoner families need to be more included, their voices given space to be heard in a manner that influences action and initiatives and helps to remove their current positionality as 'silent victims'.

Reflection points

- Could you adopt the term 'silent victims' in your own work and, if so, how might this help respond to some of the challenges facing prisoners' loved ones?
- How might we shift public perceptions and narratives about prisoners' families to help improve their visibility and experiences?
- How and why should the experiences of prisoners' families be viewed through both a cultural and gendered lens?
- We recommend more inter-agency work to support prisoners' families – in this chapter how have we demonstrated the benefits of doing this at Himaya Haven?

Notes

[1] Community Interest Company.
[2] Please see Buncy et al (2022) for a critical discussion of this term.
[3] As is the case globally.
[4] 'Adverse childhood experiences (ACEs) are potentially traumatic events that can have negative, lasting effects on health and well-being. These experiences range from physical, emotional, or sexual abuse to parental divorce or the incarceration of a parent or guardian' (Child Trends, 2014, p 1).
[5] For more information, see http://himayahaven.co.uk/
[6] This is a benefit people receive in the UK if they are unemployed or work less than 16 hours per week.

References

Abass, T. (2015) Cultural Consequences – The Lived Experiences and Support Needs of British Pakistanis with a Family Member in Prison, Doctoral dissertation, Huddersfield: University of Huddersfield.

Abass, T., Carla, R and Raikes, B. (2016) Breaking down barriers: understanding the experience of British Pakistani families affected by imprisonment, [online]. Available from: http://eprints.hud.ac.uk/id/eprint/28478/1/Breakingpercent20down percent20Barriers percent20pre-proofs.pdf [Accessed: 2 November 2020].

Arditti, J.A., Joest, K.S., Lambert-Shute, J. and Walker, L. (2010) The role of emotions in fieldwork: a self-study of family research in a corrections setting, *The Qualitative Report*, 15(6), 1387–414.

Arooj (2017) Reducing offending within BAME and Muslim communities, [online]. Available from: www.arooj.org.uk/wp-content/uploads/2019/02/AROOJ-RESEARCH-REVISED-NAPO-Version-OCT-2017.pdf [Accessed: 24 February 2021].

Barnard, H. (2014) Tackling poverty across all ethnicities in the UK, [online] 26 August. Available from: www.jrf.org.uk/report/tackling-poverty-acr oss-all-ethnicities-uk [Accessed: 24 November 2020].

Bell, C. (2021) *Himaya Haven Project Evaluation Report 2021: Supporting BAME Families of Prisoners*. Unpublished report. Available from Himaya Haven CIC on request.

Bibi, R.S. (2020) Himaya Haven: report and statement of accounts 1st April 2018–31st March 2019 and 1st April 2019–31st March 2020, [online] August. Available from: https://drive.google.com/file/d/1MBTqaCil neWyL269kgnNTQV-1qd9t7yE/view [Accessed: 23 September 2021].

Bibi, R.S. (2021a) Prisoners' families: the silent victims on the outside, [online] 21 May. Available from: www.desiblitz.com/content/prisoners-families-the-silent-victims-on-the-outside [Accessed: 17 June 2021].

Bibi, R.S (2021b) 15 challenges facing British Asian women, [online] 6 September. Available from: www.desiblitz.com/content/15-challenges-fac ing-british-asian-women [Accessed: 28 September 2021].

Booth, N. (2020) *Maternal Imprisonment and Family Life: From the Caregiver's Perspectives*, Bristol: Policy Press.

Booth, N. and Masson, I. (2021) Loved ones of remand prisoners: the hidden victims of COVID-19, *Prison Service Journal*, 253, 23–31.

Booth, N. and Masson, I. with Dakri, F. (2022) (Wo)men in the middle: the gendered role of supporting prisoners, in Masson, I. and Booth, N. (eds.) *The Routledge Handbook of Women's Experiences of Criminal Justice*, Abingdon: Routledge, pp 413–23.

Brynin, M. and Longhi, S. (2015) The effect of occupation on poverty among ethnic minority groups, [online] March. Available from: www. jrf.org.uk/sites/default/files/jrf/migrated/files/occupation-poverty-eth nic-minority-full.pdf [Accessed: 24 November 2020].

Buncy, S, Bradley, A., and Goodwin, S. (2022) Muslim women moving on from crime in I. Masson and N. Booth (eds.) *The Routledge Handbook of Women's Experiences of Criminal Justice*, Abingdon: Routledge, pp 137–48.

Cambridge Dictionary (2021) Victim, [online]. Available from: https://dictionary.cambridge.org/dictionary/english/victim [Accessed: 24 February 2021].

Child Trends (2014) Research brief: adverse childhood experiences, [online] July. Available from: www.childtrends.org/wp-content/uploads/2014/07/Brief-adverse-childhood-experiences_FINAL.pdf [Accessed: 22 September 2021].

Codd, H. (2008) *In the Shadow of Prison: Families, Imprisonment and Criminal Justice*, London: Willan Publishing.

Comfort, M. (2009) 'We share everything we can the best way we can'. Sustaining romance across prison walls, [online]. Available from: http://transatlantica.revues.org/4281 [Accessed: 24 February 2021].

Condry, R. (2007) *Families Shamed: The Consequences of Crime for Relatives of Serious Offenders*, London: Willan Publishers.

Cunningham, A. and Linda, R. (2003) *Waiting for Mommy: Giving a Voice to the Hidden Victims of Imprisonment*, London: Centre for Children and Families in the Justice System.

Dickie, D. (2013) The financial impact of imprisonment on families, [online]. Available from: www.familiesoutside.org.uk/content/uploads/2013/10/financial-impact-imprisonmentfamilies.pdf [Accessed: 24 February 2021].

Farmer, M. (2017) The importance of strengthening prisoners' family ties to prevent reoffending and reduce intergenerational crime by Lord Farmer, [online]. Available from: https://assets.publishing.service.gov.uk/government/uploads/system/uploads/attachment_data/file/642244/farmer-review-report.pdf [Accessed: 24 February 2021].

Ganeshpanchan, Z. and Masson, I. (2021) Harmful social and cultural practices that exist within South Asian communities in the UK and their impact on women, in Masson, I., Baldwin, L. and Booth, N. (eds.) *Critical Reflections on Women, Family, Crime, and Justice*, Policy Press: Bristol, pp 35–56.

Hames, C. and Pedreira, D. (2003) Children with parents in prison: disenfranchised grievers who benefit from bibliotherapy, *Illness, Crisis and Loss*, 11, 377–86.

Hannem, S.N. (2008) Marked by Association: Stigma, Marginalisation, Gender and the Families of Male Prisoners in Canada, PhD thesis, Carleton University: Ottawa.

Hough, C.V. (2017) Transforming rehabilitation: a critical evaluation of barriers encountered by an offender rehabilitation program for South Asian/Muslim offenders within the new probation service model, in Riciardelli, R. and Peters, A.M.F. (eds.) *After Prison: Navigating Employment and Reintegration*, Waterloo, Ontario: Wilfrid Laurier University Press, pp 159–80.

Horowitz, M.J. (1986) Stress-response syndromes: post-traumatic and adjustment disorders, *Psychiatry*, 1, 409–24.

Jardine, C. (2018) Constructing and maintaining family in the context of imprisonment, *British Journal of Criminology*, 58, 114–31.

Jones, A., Gallagher, B., Manby, M., Robertson, O. and Schutzwohl, M. (2013) *Children of Prisoners: Interventions and Mitigations to Strengthen Mental Health*, Huddersfield: University of Huddersfield.

Jones, A. (2021) What are the challenges and opportunities for schools in supporting children of people in prison?, in Masson, I., Baldwin, L. and Booth, N. (eds.) *Critical Reflections on Women, Family, Crime, and Justice*, Bristol: Policy Press, pp 129–52.

Kincaid, S., Roberts, M. and Kane, E. (2019) Children of prisoners: fixing a broken system, [online] February. Available from: www.nicco.org.uk/userfi les/downloads/5c90a6395f6d8-children-of-prisoners-full-report-web-vers ion.pdf [Accessed: 1 June 2021].

Kotova, A. (2014) Justice and prisoners' families. Howard League. What is justice?, [online]. Available from: https://howardleague.org/wp-content/ uploads/2016/04/HLWP_5_2014_2.pdf [Accessed: 26 August 2021].

Lammy, D. (2017) The Lammy Review: an independent review into the treatment of, and outcomes for, Black, Asian and Minority Ethnic individuals in the criminal justice system, [online]. Available from: https:// assets.publishing.service.gov.uk/government/uploads/system/uploads/ attachment_data/file/643001/lammy-review-final-report.pdf [Accessed: 5 November 2020].

Lockwood, K. and Raikes, B. (2015) A difficult disclosure: the dilemmas faced by families affected by parental imprisonment regarding what information to share, in Reeves, C. (ed.) *Experiencing Imprisonment: Research on the Experience of Living and Working in Carceral Institutions*, London: Routledge.

MacPherson, W. (1999) The Stephen Lawrence Inquiry: report of an inquiry, [online] February. Available from: https://assets.publishing.service.gov. uk/government/uploads/system/uploads/attachment_data/file/277111/ 4262.pdf [Accessed: 24 February 2021].

Mahmood, T. and Mohammad, H. (2014) *Arooj: Reducing Offending within South Asian/Muslim Communities – A Research report*, UK: Arooj [Available on request].

Masson, I. (2019) *Incarcerating Motherhood: The Enduring Harms of First Short Periods of Imprisonment on Mothers*, Abingdon: Routledge.

Masson, I. and Booth, N. (2018) Examining prisoners' families: definitions, developments and difficulties, *Howard League for Penal Reform ECAN Bulletin*, 39, 15–20.

Masson, I. and Booth, N. (2022) Using techniques of neutralisation to maintain contact: the experiences of loved ones supporting remand prisoners, *The Howard Journal of Crime and Justice*, 61 (4), 463–83.

Matthews, J. (1983) *Forgotten Victims: How Prison Affects the Family*, London: National Association for the Care and Resettlement of Offenders.

Ministry of Justice (MoJ) and Department for Children, Schools, and Families (DCSF) (2007) Children of offenders review, [online]. Available from: www.nicco.org.uk/userfiles/downloads/012%20-%20Child ren%20of%20Offenders%20Review%202007%20MoJ.pdf [Accessed: 23 September 2021].

MoJ (2021) Prisoner population statistics, [online] 8 January. Available from: www.gov.uk/government/statistics/prison-population-figures-2021 [Accessed: 20 May 2021].

Murray, J. and Farrington, D.P. (2005) Parental imprisonment: effects on boys' antisocial behaviour and delinquency through the life course, *Journal of Child Psychology and Psychiatry*, 46, 1269–78.

Raikes, B. (2014) Prisons without walls, *Every Child Journal*, 4(3), 20–7.

Robertson, O., Christmann, K., Sharratt, K., Berman, H.A., Manby, M., Ayre, E., Foca, L., Asiminei, R., Philbrick, K. and Gavriluta, C. (2016) *Children of Prisoners: Their Situation and Role in Long-Term Crime Prevention*, [online]. Available from: https://eprints.hud.ac.uk/id/eprint/28911/1/Children percent20of percent20prisoners_version percent20accepted percent20for percent20publication.pdf [Accessed: 24 November 2020].

Robinson, G., McLean, R. and Densley, J. (2019) Working county lines: child criminal exploitation and illicit drug dealing in Glasgow and Merseyside, *International Journal of Offender Therapy and Comparative Criminology*, 63(5), 694–711.

Sharp, S.F., Marcus-Mendoza, S.T., Bentley, R.G., Simpson, D.B. and Love, S.R. (1997) Gender differences in the impact of incarceration on the children and families of drug offenders, *Journal of the Oklahoma Criminal Justice Research Consortium*, 4.

Shaw, R. (1992) *Imprisoned Fathers and the Orphans of Justice*, London: Routledge.

Singh, S. (n.d.) Coping with divorce as a British Asian woman, [online]. Available from: www.desiblitz.com/content/coping-with-divorce-as-a-british-asian-woman [Accessed: 28 September 2021].

Smith, R., Grimshaw, R., Romeo, R. and Knapp, M. (2017) Poverty and disadvantage among prisoners' families, [online]. Available from: www.jrf.org.uk/sites/default/files/jrf/migrated/files/2003-poverty-prisoners-families.pdf [Accessed: 24 February 2021].

Toor, S. (2009) British Asian girls, crime and youth justice. *Youth Justice*, 9(3), 239–253.

Turney, K. (2018) Adverse childhood experiences among children of incarcerated parents, *Children and Youth Services Review*, 89, 218–25.

Winder, B., Blagden, N., Armitage, R., Duncan, K., Wakeham, A., Roberts, L. and Berti, C. (2020) The experiences of non-offending partners of individuals who have committed sexual offences: recommendations for practitioners and stakeholders, [online] November. Available from: http://irep.ntu.ac.uk/id/eprint/41769/1/1392554_Winder.pdf [Accessed: 24 February 2021].

Windle, J., Moyle, L. and Coomber, R. (2020) 'Vulnerable' kids going country: children and young people's involvement in county lines drug dealing, *Youth Justice*, 20(1–2), 64–78.

PART II

Violence, abuse and justice

5

Recognising and responding to domestic violence and abuse in LGB and/or T+ people's relationships: towards a 'relationships services' approach

Rebecca Barnes and Catherine Donovan

Introduction

The last two decades have seen significant changes across the UK and internationally in the visibility, social acceptability and legal recognition of lesbian, gay, bisexual and/or transgender (LGB and/or T+[1]) people's relationships and families (Weeks, 2007). Significant milestones have included the expansion of equality legislation concerning sexuality and gender reassignment, the criminalisation of hate crime motivated by sexual orientation or transgender identity and legalisation of same-sex marriage in all nations of the UK (Stonewall, 2021). Legal change does not necessarily bring social and cultural change; however, the British Social Attitudes Survey, 2018 found that 66 per cent of the 2,884 people surveyed said that same-sex relationships were 'not wrong at all' compared with just 11 per cent in 1987 (Curtice et al, 2019). The benefits of these changes are, however, unevenly distributed, with LGB and/or T+ working-class people (McDermott, 2011) and people of colour (Stonewall, 2018) remaining marginalised both within and outside of LGB and/or T+ spaces.

This wider affirmation of the validity and integrity of LGB and/or T+ people's intimate relationships coincides with growing evidence of domestic violence and abuse (DVA) among LGB and/or T+ people (Renzetti, 1992; Ristock, 2002; Finneran and Stephenson, 2013; Donovan and Hester, 2014, 2010; Badenes-Ribera et al, 2016; Donovan and Barnes, 2020a; Rogers, 2021). Estimates of the prevalence of DVA among LGB and/or T+ populations have primarily been based on non-random, self-selected survey samples. This has resulted in very variable and high estimates of DVA victimisation, ranging from 9.6 to 51.5 per cent for women (Badenes-Ribera et al, 2016) and 29.7 to 78.0 per cent for men (Finneran and Stephenson, 2013). Bisexual, transgender and non-binary people have often been excluded. More recently, the inclusion of sexuality (but rarely gender identity) questions in national, random surveys of DVA have enabled more comparable estimates with heterosexual people to be calculated. Analysis of Crime Survey for England and Wales data has found that bisexual women are almost twice as likely (10.9 per cent) to report having experienced DVA in the last 12 months, compared with 6 per cent of heterosexual women, and 8 per cent of gay/lesbian women (ONS, 2018; see also Messinger, 2011 for comparable differences in the United States).

SafeLives' (2018) Insights data – based on case file data from 754 LGBT+ service users – reveals that LGBT+ victims/survivors report significantly higher rates of physical and sexual abuse and are almost twice as likely to have attempted suicide. While earlier DVA research speculated that coercive control would not occur in same-sex relationships, due to the supposed absence of gendered power differentials (Stark, 2007), this suggestion has been refuted by empirical studies (Ristock, 2002; Donovan and Hester, 2014; Frankland and Brown, 2014). Johnson's (2006) typology of intimate partner violence (IPV) distinguishes between different types of IPV, including coercively controlling violence, situational couple violence and violent resistance. The Coral Project research found that this typology resonates with LGB and/or T+ people's use and experience of abusive behaviours too (Donovan and Barnes, 2020a).

What distinguishes LGB and/or T+ DVA from heterosexual, cisgender[2] women's experiences of DVA is the structural backdrop of heteronormativity, cisnormativity and homo/bi/transphobia (Donovan and Barnes, 2020b). Heteronormativity is the assumption that all relationships are between a man and a woman and that this is the only or most acceptable relationship form. Cisnormativity is the assumption that everyone is either female or male, and that their biological sex and gender identity are coherent. Cisnormativity therefore marginalises people who are transgender or who identify with no gender or multiple gender identities, for example, those who define as non-binary or gender-fluid. These structural issues influence whether LGB and/or T+ people feel accepted and supported, and whether they can 'come out' and live openly as an LGB and/or T+ person and with what consequences (Balsam, 2001). They also impact upon whether LGB and/or T+ people feel that they would be safe, respected and understood if they seek help for relationship difficulties, including DVA (SafeLives, 2018; Donovan and Barnes, 2020b).

These barriers to help seeking are compounded by the 'public story of DVA'. This is the dominant societal image of DVA which involves a bigger, stronger, male perpetrator and a smaller, weaker, female victim, and is characterised by physical violence (Donovan and Hester, 2010). The public story contributes to LGB and/or T+ people not being aware that DVA can happen in their relationships, as well as thinking that DVA services would not cater for them (Donovan and Hester, 2014; Donovan and Barnes,

2020a). Consequently, LGB and/or T+ victims/survivors seldom access specialist DVA services[3] and rarely report to the police (Ristock, 2002; Donovan and Hester, 2014). Instead, they most often seek help from friends or from counsellors/psychotherapists, whether privately or via NHS mental health services (Donovan and Hester, 2014; Donovan and Barnes, 2020b). There is a need for specialist DVA services to become more inclusive and visible (SafeLives, 2018), and for improved resourcing of the few specialist LGB and/or T+ DVA services in the UK (Donovan and Butterby, 2020). However, there is another issue. The Coral Project survey highlighted that while the experience and use of abusive behaviours were widely reported, many cases would fall below the threshold for specialist DVA services, not least because of their limited resources. This has been argued to be the case for heterosexual women's experiences of DVA too (Radford and Gill, 2006).

This chapter focuses on how to support LGB and/or T+ people who are experiencing or perpetrating DVA and who may, but often may not, be at the threshold for a specialist DVA or criminal justice intervention. In particular, data from focus groups with different groups of practitioners is unpacked to make sense of these needs and how occupational culture and their dominant client group shaped understandings of our earlier survey and interview data and conceptualisations of DVA. This analysis supports the case for a more holistic, LGBT-inclusive relationship services approach to increase access to relationship support and, where appropriate, DVA interventions. This, in turn, would improve the safety and quality of LGB and/or T+ people's intimate relationships and family lives.

Methods

This chapter is based on the analysis of qualitative data from eight focus groups with a broad range of practitioners, conducted as part of the wider ESRC-funded Coral Project (2012–14). This was the first UK study to focus on understanding LGB and/or T+ perpetrators of DVA. Ethical approval was secured by the principal investigator through their university ethics committee. This mixed-methods project also included a UK-wide survey of LGB and/or T+ people which explored 'what they do when things go wrong' in their relationships (n=872). Thirty-six volunteers from the survey who had reported using 'abusive'[4] behaviours in an intimate relationship were interviewed, as were 23 practitioners in perpetrator services (primarily for heterosexual men), either in the community or in the criminal justice system (CJS) (see Donovan et al, 2014 or Donovan and Barnes, 2020a for full methodology).

In the final component of the study, focus groups were held with practitioners to discuss the findings from our survey and interviews with LGB and/or T+ people with them. Rather than restricting the sample to specialist perpetrator practitioners, practitioners from multiple statutory, voluntary and private services which work with LGB and/or T+ people and have a direct or indirect role in offering relationships advice or support were invited. Eight focus groups were held with 53 participants: six focus groups took place in England, one in Scotland and one in Wales. Separate groups were conducted with:

- DVA practitioners
- probation and perpetrator services
- LGB and/or T+ identified or affirmative counsellors and psychotherapists
- relationship and family counsellors and therapists
- youth workers
- education professionals whose remit includes formal or informal sex and relationships education
- men's services
- voluntary sector services with various remits.

Participants were invited to offer their perspectives on the earlier findings and case studies from the interviews, and to reflect on their own work with LGB and/or T+ people. They were also asked about their training and infrastructure needs. All focus groups were audio-recorded, externally transcribed and then checked by the focus group facilitator for accuracy. The data was analysed thematically.

Findings

Three key themes were identified. The first examines the way in which practitioners – especially those within specialist DVA victim/survivor and perpetrator services – understood DVA largely through the lens of the 'public story' of DVA (Donovan and Hester, 2010) and focused on the highest risk cases, in other words, the crisis response (Hodes and Mennicke, 2019). This contrasted with the approaches and understandings adopted by counselling and psychotherapy practitioners, considered in the second theme. Here, practitioners embraced more fluid approaches to understanding victim/perpetrator roles, and more individualistic rather than structural understandings of DVA. The third theme considers how a more holistic, multi-agency, relationships services approach could open up more spaces for LGB and/or T+ people to talk about their relationship difficulties and receive appropriate, safe and inclusive support.

Relationships in crisis: the DVA response

Practitioners delivering the DVA crisis response were mainly but not exclusively in two of the eight focus groups. These were specialist DVA workers for victims/survivors (Independent Domestic Violence Advisers (IDVAs), outreach workers, refuge workers), one police representative, probation officers and practitioners who deliver DVA perpetrator interventions, either in probation or in voluntary services. Their client group were, typically, some of the most high-risk DVA cases, and for probation staff, only those within the CJS. Most had only encountered a small number of LGB and/or T+ victims/survivors or perpetrators, with the exceptions being two IDVAs for male victims/survivors who regularly worked with men in same-sex relationships.

It is perhaps not surprising, therefore, that most DVA practitioners understood DVA as largely framed by the public story of DVA, that is, a dominant or exclusive focus on female victim/survivors and male perpetrators, expectations of high levels of physical and sexual violence, an assessment of high risk of lethal harm and delineation of clear victim/survivor and perpetrator roles, grounded in an analysis of power and control. For example: "Yeah, a lot of the recent ones I've had have been quite severe physical violence. Using an axe was one of the, the most recent one and, aye, a lot of physical violence really" (Tess,[5] DVA services focus group). Many of these practitioners, therefore, considered that the levels and types of violence and abuse most commonly reported in our study were rather low, for example:

'I mean that, I think these figures seem quite low to, these percentages seem, I don't know, maybe it's because I'm a bit, um, been doing this job for too long, but these per cent, I know these are general responses aren't they, but they seem like quite low percentages really to me.' (Libby, voluntary sector focus group)

Some practitioners acknowledged that their expectations of very high levels of physical violence are grounded in their client group comprising of the minority of perpetrators who come to the attention of the police and social services. This reflects Johnson's (2006) DVA research which finds that criminal justice and refuge samples of heterosexual women victims/survivors predominantly experience coercively controlling violence (CCV, or 'intimate terrorism'), characterised by more severe, entrenched violence underpinned by control. In the general population, the lower-level, more episodic situational couple violence (SCV) is most reported. Although SCV is less likely than CCV to escalate, Johnson found that it did in 28 per cent of cases (Johnson, 2006, p 1010). Therefore, while SCV does not require the same response as CCV, it would still benefit from an intervention (Tavistock Centre, 2016; Hodes and Mennicke, 2019). It was perhaps surprising, therefore, that specialist DVA practitioners generally did not raise the possibility of early intervention to interrupt the possible escalation of episodic violence and abuse.

Grounded in feminist analyses of DVA (Johnson, 2006; Stark, 2007), specialist DVA practitioners were most likely to position power and control as being central to DVA, and to consider abusive relationships as characterised by an asymmetry of power. This understanding guided views about how to assess who the victim/survivor and who the perpetrator is in an abusive relationship. Participants highlighted the need to attend to, for example, "who's the person who's instigating what's going on?" (Gina, DVA services focus group) and "who's setting the rules and, and who's feeling the fear basically" (Lana, DVA services focus group). Some practitioners were aware that the existing heteronormative tools for assessing relationships may not fully capture LGB and/or T+ people's experiences (see further discussion in Donovan, 2013). This led some practitioners to speak of the need to broaden the public story to recognise other forms of power besides gender (for example, age, sexuality, socio-economic status) and to acknowledge the potential risks of referring both partners in a same-sex relationship to a perpetrator programme.

In contrast, potential support needs for relationships where the violence and abuse are not grounded in coercive control were seldom discussed, suggesting that these specialist DVA practitioners largely saw this as sitting outside of their remit. There were some exceptions: two participants acknowledged the need for support and intervention even where the risk of serious harm was lower. One participant in the DVA services focus group, Fiona, indicated that her service would support someone even if they did not meet the "textbook definition" of coercive control. However, funding pressures typically manufacture a need to ration resources and prioritise cases where the risk of harm is highest (Radford and Gill, 2006; Stanley and Humphreys, 2014), leaving a gap of support for lower-risk cases which would benefit from early intervention (Robinson and Payton, 2016). Rather than approaching specialist DVA services, Coral Project survey respondents were much more likely to have sought help from counselling/psychotherapy. It is apt, therefore, to consider this practice setting next.

Individualising relationship troubles: counselling responses

Counsellors and psychotherapists are especially important for LGB and/or T+ people who are experiencing DVA (Ristock, 2002; Donovan and Hester, 2014; Donovan and Barnes, 2020b), perhaps due to barriers to accessing statutory services and more limited use of family for informal help seeking (SafeLives, 2018; Donovan and Barnes, 2020b). There is a debate in the specialist DVA sector between those who believe that couples' therapy is very risky where there is a significant imbalance of power and control (Trute, 1998; Tomsich et al, 2015) and those who believe that, by not treating all violence and abuse as homogenous, counselling can provide a useful way of challenging male violence within a relationship context where both wish to stay together (Wendt et al, 2020). The Tavistock Centre (2016) in the UK suggest, for example, that situational couple violence could potentially be addressed via couples counselling, unlike CCV. We were interested in understanding how relationship counsellors and psychotherapists worked with LGB and/or T+ clients where there is potential or unequivocal DVA, and how they negotiated risk and safety.

One of our focus groups comprised of counsellors/psychotherapists who identified as LGB and/or T+ themselves or openly described themselves as being LGBT+ affirmative. All of these practitioners were working as private, self-employed therapists. Another focus group comprised of counsellors/psychotherapists who specialised in relationship counselling, although some offered a combination of one-to-one and relationship/family therapy. This group had more mixed practice settings: from self-employed therapists in private practice, to third-sector relationships or family support organisations. Across the two groups, some had extensive therapeutic experience with DVA, while others did not. Participants held a broad range of different counselling philosophies shaping how they approached their work and, for some, their attitudes towards practices such as risk assessment and signposting to other agencies.

In contrast with many of the specialist DVA practitioners who, in the majority, understood DVA as a structural issue that reflects wider gender and (sometimes) other structural inequalities, this was a minority position among the counselling/psychotherapy participants. While some acknowledged structural factors such as poverty, in the main their prime emphasis was on relationship dynamics or the individual psyche. This meant a less structural approach to abusive relationships and greater focus on the development of patterns of behaviour which can give rise to power imbalances and maladaptive behaviours in intimate relationships. Lydia explained: "I'm a Gestalt psychotherapist so my perspective is that these things are co-created so that there is a, there isn't a one person's doing all of this, that actually both parties respond to each other in a, they respond to each other, so it happens relationally" (Lydia, relationship counselling focus group). Lydia's explanation, echoing several other participants', views patterns of behaviour that have developed through a systemic and relational lens, that is, understanding how the behaviour of both partners has contributed to relationship struggles (see Hansen, 1993; Hattendorf, 1997). This suggests that people are not abusive or controlling in their own right but rather in response to the behaviour of their partner. Rather than drawing on the language of coercive control, many counselling/psychotherapy participants talked about provocation, persecution and unconscious power play. Unlike specialist DVA practitioners who tended to consider perpetrators' behaviour to be intentional, some counsellors/

psychotherapists were less convinced that negative behaviours would be consciously enacted.

These conceptualisations of violence and abuse in intimate relationships gave rise to a greater sense of fluidity around the roles of victim/survivor and perpetrator, or the avoidance of these terms. In contrast with the DVA crisis response, where victim/survivors are considered to be predominantly disempowered, some of the counsellors and psychotherapists considered that occupying a victim role might be a position of power in a relationship, by virtue of being able to exercise the upper hand morally or to get one's own way by repeatedly bringing up the other partner's transgressions. This is illustrated by the following exchange involving multiple participants in the LGBT+ counselling and psychotherapy focus group:

Nina: And I'm just thinking too about one of my clients, ah, the victim can be incredibly powerful. Um, that victim position can drive the other [laughs] to violence.

Nigel: Sure, it can be provoking.

Katy: I think violence can very often be fear-based for people, and so a variety of the other person's behaviours may have triggered some reaction, which doesn't make it okay, but it's also thinking about that whole dynamic of what it means for each partner.

Bev: And it can also give power because whatever behaviours or points or grievances or difficulties the person has had prior to that aggressive behaviour, that's now dismissed. Anything that, you know, may be valid about what they were bringing will, 'None of that counts anymore because you were aggressive'. Um.

Sam: Dismissed.

Consequently, partners are encouraged to accept responsibility for how their actions and words have affected the other, with a need for deep reflection to recognise recurrent patterns of behaviour or thinking. The purpose of therapy is therefore to facilitate a space where people can gain insight into their behaviours and how they impact on others. As Sylvia stated,

'It's not about blame, it's about allowing somebody to say, "What is it about me that leaves me in a position of being bullied? What is it about me that has led me to be the one who's constantly picked on? What is it that I do?" And to be able to interrogate that and to find out what it was at stake that left you doing those things, more than once usually.' (Sylvia, relationship counselling focus group)

Through the lens of a feminist DVA response, these approaches would widely be considered to be victim blaming, reinforcing the perpetrator's typical insistence that they are driven to do something in response to the victim's/survivor's behaviour (Hansen, 1993; Hattendorf, 1997). Therefore, while there are situations where working in such ways could be enlightening and empowering for clients, careful assessment of how power is operating in the relationship should be a fundamental prerequisite to embarking on therapy.

For some participants, a non-directive and non-judgemental approach was core to their counselling philosophy. For these practitioners, risk assessment or safety planning were conceptualised as "bureaucratic" processes that might undermine the therapeutic relationship and, as one practitioner suggested, result in the therapist becoming seen as a "persecutor". Different protocols appeared to exist between self-employed therapists and those working for agencies. Sam reflected on risk management as posing a dilemma for therapists:

'Um managing risk? … It's a confidential activity, psychotherapy, so are you going to be using the same protection measures as you would if you're working outside of that context? … Do we say, "We, we'll breach confidentiality if you're going to continue to, to beat your partner"? Um and I'm not saying I have an answer to that.' (Sam, LGB and/or T+ counsellors and psychotherapists focus group)

Some private counsellors and psychotherapists considered safety planning to be an important part of their role, especially when working with victims/survivors. Bev, in the LGB and/or T+ counsellors and psychotherapists focus group, explained that she made clients aware of relevant agencies and helped them to identify "at what point in time would you know that you're in danger … what would have to happen for you to say, 'this is now something I no longer see within the realms of, um, a safe, acceptable relationship'?" – and then reminding them when these limits have been passed. Others spoke about helping clients to consider how to address basic needs, such as safe housing.

Risk assessment was particularly topical in relation to couples' work. More formal processes existed for therapists working within larger agencies, particularly those working mainly with families referred via social services, rather than private clients. As Jenny explained:

'I think part of our risk assessment with couples, if there has been violence, is thinking "will the therapy itself in the short term raise the likelihood of more violence?" [others agreeing]. And I, I think it does sometimes, so that needs thinking about carefully. And something about at the end of sessions, like what state you send people off into.' (Jenny, relationship counselling focus group)

However, some practitioners seemed reluctant to adopt a more holistic focus on people's circumstances, for fear that this would jeopardise the therapeutic work. As Sylvia said:

'I think there's something about, ahh, a particular orientation of always leaving the power with the person who's coming to see me, and trying not to fall into a place of saying "you need to do that, you should do that, you might, you need to go there".' (Sylvia, relationships counselling focus group)

These contrasting perspectives point to a lack of consensus in counsellors' and psychotherapists' understanding of DVA, risk assessment and safety planning, and would merit more comprehensive research. It is also crucial to recognise that counselling is not readily accessible: private counselling is financially prohibitive for many, especially working-class people; while NHS mental health services are heavily rationed and may lack competence in understanding LGB and/or T+ lives (Barnes et al, 2021).

Towards relationship services: promoting early intervention and positive relationships

Thus far we have considered practitioners working in the specialist DVA sector and counselling and psychotherapy practitioners. Among other practitioners, such as those engaged in non-DVA voluntary sector organisations, sex and relationships education or youth work, understandings of DVA that emphasised power and control were most frequently expressed. However, the depth of their understanding of LGB and/or T+ lives varied, and some were not sure where to refer people experiencing DVA, especially when these clients did not fit neatly within the public story of DVA. Their role in being part of a holistic response to LGB and/or T+ DVA has been under-explored.

This final theme draws on our observations from the focus groups that within a much broader practitioner base, there is significant knowledge, insight and opportunity to provide relationships support and education. Harnessing this expertise and opportunity would enhance early intervention and the promotion of positive relationships, both widening the pool of people who receive relationships support and signposting and preventing the escalation of risk and need to the point that they require a crisis response. Importantly, we are not calling for these practitioners to become experts in DVA or in intimate relationships; however, some already provide formal or informal relationships support but may have gaps in their knowledge regarding DVA or LGB and/or T+ lives.

A relationship services approach is not something that most participants suggested or explicitly identified with, but rather it brings together numerous recurring themes within their responses. It also responds to other key findings within the Coral Project. Our survey found that while most perpetration of abusive behaviours fell below the threshold of CCV, many participants recognised the need to change their behaviour in relationships: 37 per cent strongly agreed/agreed that 'My behaviour is a problem sometimes' and 15 per cent strongly agreed/agreed that 'I am at the stage where I should think about changing my behaviour'. Of the 872 respondents, almost a quarter identified having a problem with needing to be in control, and more than a sixth reported having anger issues. These needs were further reinforced in interviews with survey respondents, some participants expressing apprehension about entering subsequent relationships and worrying about repeating previous patterns of problematic or harmful behaviour (Donovan and Barnes, 2020a).

What remains unaddressed, however, is where these LGB and/or T+ people would go to get advice and support with these issues. As noted earlier, the dominant heteronormative and cisnormative approaches of mainstream services mean that LGB and/or T+ people are frequently wary of services not understanding them or their relationships and/or responding in homo/bi/transphobic ways (Donovan and Barnes, 2020b). Further, intimate relationships and experiences of DVA among LGB and/or T+ people – and particularly those of bisexual (Head and Milton, 2014) and transgender (Rogers, 2021) people continue to be marginalised and invisibilised. This reduces opportunities to talk about relationship issues and may lead to difficulties being concealed. As Nigel, in the LGB and/or T+ counselling and psychotherapy focus group, stated, "we have an identity which we have to protect because everybody else is attacking it".

The characteristics of a relationship services approach can be summarised as follows. Firstly, *a relationships service approach needs to be framed around support for intimate relationships, rather than around DVA*. This might mean focusing the messaging on 'positive relationships', relationship troubleshooting or developing relationship skills, as Nigel suggested: "Sure, and call it something new, less inflammatory, like ... skills for managing conflict in relationships could be a much more neutral, less pathologising kind of, because every relationship's going to have conflict [others indicating agreement]" (Nigel, LGB and/or T+ counselling and psychotherapy focus group). Similarly, Laura and Liz in the youth work focus group both talked about the need to foreground a positive slant on LGB and/or T+ relationships, therefore focusing messages on what loving, equal relationships look like:

Laura: I think ... we have an opportunity to inflate positive relationships and sell ... what a positive relationship is, rather than go down the route [of] 'Right okay, it's abuse, it's a negative, the world's a pit, everybody out there's a potential perpetrator and watch yourself, watch your back', doesn't sell, it doesn't sell positive relationships to the gay community.

Liz: And it doesn't empower.

Focusing on positive LGB and/or T+ relationships or normalising the need to develop relationship skills are also important political acts to destigmatise LGB and/or T+ people's relationships.

Youth work, schools-based sex and relationships education, youth offending services and young people's mental health and homelessness services need to be central to a preventative relationship services approach. Being in a first relationship as an LGB and/or T+ person is a risk factor for DVA (Ristock, 2002; Donovan and Hester, 2014; Donovan and Barnes, 2020a; 2020b). Abusive LGB and/or T+ partners can wield 'experiential power' over a victim/survivor who is newly out or not yet out, exploiting the wider lack of opportunity to discuss what relationships and sex look like for LGB and/or T+ people by dictating relationship and sexual expectations (Donovan and Barnes, 2020a; 2020b). While all young people need to learn relationship skills and be equipped to recognise the signs of harmful or controlling relationships, there is a particular need for LGB and/or T+ relationships and positive relationship role models to be more visible.

Taking the emphasis away from DVA and normalising talking about good relationships is also necessary because many LGB and/or T+ people do not recognise DVA and do not consider DVA specialist services as being appropriate to them (Donovan and Hester, 2010). Megan (voluntary sector focus group) suggested that information about support for relationships needed to be available in the spaces which LGB and/or T+ people frequent as a matter of course – workplaces, GP surgeries and dentists, for example – and not to assume that all LGB and/or T+ people would be part of local LGB and/or T+ social or support networks.

Secondly, *relationship services could operate a triage approach whereby an assessment of risk and need leads partners to be appropriately referred and supported.* This would promote early intervention and prevent the potential escalation of violence and abuse. Some practitioners highlight a need for more services that are accessible to all, rather than only being available to the highest-risk victims/survivors via – most frequently – a police or social services referral. This is important to target the aforementioned gap in support for lower-risk cases which fall below the threshold of CCV. Several participants suggested that more online advice and support for LGB and/or T+ people and their intimate relationships would be valuable, such as tools to help people to assess whether their behaviour might be abusive.

Careful identification of the type of intimate partner violence and the power and control dynamics in a relationship could lead to better identification of which couples might benefit from couples counselling and which would not (Tavistock Centre, 2016). Such an approach, however, is contingent on relationships services being connected to appropriate and LGB and/or T+-inclusive specialist DVA services. Currently, a key challenge is the lack of availability and under-resourcing of specialist victim/survivor (Donovan and Butterby, 2020) and perpetrator (Barnes and Donovan, 2016) interventions to LGB and/or T+ people, and the lack of a robust evidence base to inform the design and delivery of such work.

Looking beyond existing relationships-focused provision, it is argued that there is untapped potential for crucial initial listening, opportunistic conversations and signposting to take place with a much wider range of practitioners. Megan (voluntary sector focus group), who worked in a sexual health and substance use drop-in centre, reflected that her service receives so many first-time disclosures of DVA because practitioners routinely enquire about it "every single time that we see somebody". Our data reinforces that these sorts of interactions are already taking place, for example, via practitioners in housing services, university chaplains or youth workers. However, practitioners require DVA training to build confidence about undertaking informal or formal risk assessment and safety planning.

Practitioners' knowledge and confidence could also be improved by strengthening networks between services. What we are arguing for echoes the ethos of the coordinated community response to DVA (Pence and Shephard, 1999) and multi-agency working. However, instead of relying on identifying and acting on the highest-risk cases, we envisage widening access to more holistic relationship support and early intervention (Robinson and Payton, 2016). There were instances of networking and knowledge exchange happening during the focus groups, illustrating the value of multi-agency forums and the benefits of widening membership of these to third-sector LGB and/or T+ organisations and less likely providers of relationship services.

Thirdly, *relationships services need to be grounded in an understanding of LGB and/or T+ lives and intimate relationships*. Services need to recognise the structural contexts in which LGB and/or T+ people live out their relationships, and the role of their intersecting identities (Ristock, 2002; Donovan and Barnes, 2020a; Rogers, 2021). This includes having an awareness of how homo/bi/transphobia impacts on individuals and their relationships, but without simplistically attributing DVA in LGB and/or T+ people's relationships to minority stress (see Balsam, 2001). As Carla, in the specialist DVA practitioners focus group, discussed, the history of police brutality towards LGB and/or T+ people affects their confidence to approach services without fear of discrimination (echoed in Ristock, 2002). Julia reflected that this applies to other services too and emphasised the importance of the first response being critical to building trust or deterring future disclosures: "maybe next time she will never go again and ask, you know" (Julia, specialist DVA practitioners focus group).

Numerous focus group participants recognised the heteronormativity of dominant assumptions about relationships and called for understandings of relationships which included non-monogamy or polyamory, as well as relationships organised around bondage, domination and sadomasochism (BDSM). However, participants had mixed opinions about the need for specialist LGB and/or T+ services (see also Barnes and Donovan, 2016). For example, Fiona outlined the results of a consultation that she was involved in regarding DVA services for GBT men, stating that what was important to them "was a service that specifically understood their sexual orientation … and their gender identities as gay, bisexual and trans men, so having a generic men's service was not appropriate because there's still the fears about homophobia" (Fiona, specialist DVA practitioners focus group). Amy also talked about the impact for a gay male survivor of DVA approaching her DVA agency: "It's predominantly female-run, it's run through volunteers who perhaps haven't got a great awareness of LGB and T issues … and [sighs] the perception if you walk through the door is that it is traditionally a female service for female victims of domestic violence" (Amy, men's services focus group). Key barriers that participants identified to providing more LGB and/or T+ inclusive services included the need for more comprehensive training and the lack of robust evidence to inform the development of bespoke LGB and/or T+ interventions (particularly for perpetrators of DVA).

Less often, practitioners assumed that LGB and/or T+ people would feel included in their service, without any changes being made. As Leah said, "I don't see why a lesbian woman would not feel refuge was appropriate, any more than a heterosexual woman would … I can't really see the difference" (Leah, DVA services focus group). Such 'discourses of sameness' among practitioners (Donovan and Barnes, 2019), that treating LGB and/or T+ people equally means treating them the same as heterosexual, cisgender people, risk overlooking how LGB and/or T+ people may be excluded from services that have historically, primarily, served heterosexual, cisgender people.

Conclusion

Existing interventions for relationships where there is violence and/or abuse revolve around the public story of DVA (Donovan and Hester, 2010), that is, they primarily focus on (ostensibly heterosexual, cisgender) female victims who have been abused by (ostensibly heterosexual, cisgender) male perpetrators. This has led to an unmet need for people who do not fit the public story, most notably here, LGB and/or T+ people. The public story also reifies physical violence against heterosexual, cisgender women into the risk assessment framework (Donovan, 2013), leaving an unmet need for cases of DVA at lower risk (Radford and Gill, 2006) and/or relationships where there is conflict rather than control (Hodes and Mennicke, 2019).

This understanding of DVA was evident in our analysis: most specialist DVA practitioners (including probation practitioners) considered the relationships represented in our survey and follow-up interview findings to be 'not risky enough' or 'too low' for intervention. While the partners in such relationships would not meet the threshold for intensive victim/survivor advocacy (for example, IDVA) services or the DVA perpetrator programme, there is little recognition of their need for support and intervention. In the Coral Project survey, participants themselves recognised a need to change their behaviour in relationships (Donovan and Barnes, 2020a). Early intervention is vital to enhance the quality of LGB and/or T+ people's intimate relationships, to increase awareness of DVA and to prevent escalation of lower-risk, more episodic violence and abuse into a pattern of coercive control.

The embodiment of the public story of DVA in the provision of specialist DVA services and in the understandings of LGB and/or T+ people of what DVA is means that LGB and/or T+ people seldom seek support for DVA from specialist DVA services or the police (Ristock, 2002; Donovan and Hester, 2014). Instead, they are more likely to seek out individual or couples counselling or psychotherapy (Ristock, 2002; Donovan and Hester, 2014; Donovan and Barnes, 2020b), justifying the inclusion of this practitioner group in our focus groups. Counselling and psychotherapy provide valuable insights into one's own behaviour and feelings and the behaviour of others. However, it may not be informed by an understanding of structural dimensions of power and control within and outside of people's intimate relationships (Hansen, 1993). Counsellors and psychotherapists may have limited understanding of DVA, and our analysis identified that some therapists adopted systemic approaches which would, in a specialist DVA context, be considered victim blaming (Hansen, 1993; Hattendorf, 1997). Further, we also found a lack of consensus regarding risk assessment and safety planning, with some practitioners' philosophies discouraging them from signposting clients to relevant services for fear of disempowering them or jeopardising the therapeutic relationship. Therefore, while counselling and psychotherapy are important, popular sources of support for LGB and/or T+ people, there are concerns about how well equipped practitioners are to differentiate and respond to higher-risk and need cases. There are also financial barriers to accessing counselling and psychotherapy, and high demand for low-cost or free services, inhibiting its access to all (Barnes et al, 2021).

Consequently, we argue that specialist DVA services (including relevant criminal justice agencies) and counselling and psychotherapy are two important components of a more holistic nexus of services which offer assessment, direct support, education and signposting or cross-referral to other agencies, depending on the needs and risks presented. A relationship services approach needs to take relationships and not DVA as its starting point, and be able to carefully assess how violence, abuse and power are operating in a relationship to determine which interventions would be safe and effective (Hodes and Mennicke, 2019). Rather than advocating for new services, we recommend training and stronger multi-agency relationships to facilitate opportunistic conversations and listening. Relationships services have significant potential to open up spaces for LGB and/or T+ people to talk about their relationships within services they are already likely to use. Nonetheless, many participants recognised that more work needed to be done to improve outreach to LGB and/or T+ people and to ensure that all colleagues are trained to be LGB and/or T+-inclusive.

Our argument concerns how a relationships services approach could be transformative for responses to LGB and/or T+ people's relationships, but this approach could benefit heterosexual, cisgender people too. Although specialist DVA services predominantly work with heterosexual, cisgender people (SafeLives, 2018), in reality most heterosexual, cisgender people who experience DVA in their relationships do not come into contact with these services. For example, it is estimated that fewer than 1 per cent of DVA perpetrators receive a perpetrator intervention (Home Office, 2016). Because situational couple violence is much more common than CCV among heterosexual, cisgender people too (Johnson, 2006), many of their relationships will also be below the threshold for a specialist DVA response. Providing timely access to appropriate DVA and relationship interventions is fundamental to social and criminal justice. Continued efforts to destigmatise discussion of relationship difficulties and counter the lesser visibility of LGB and/or T+ relationships and DVA will be critical to promoting earlier intervention, interrupting the cycle of abuse and promoting positive and democratic relationships.

Reflection points

- Does the public story of DVA shape your perceptions of what DVA is most likely to look like? Think about how you see DVA reported on in the news, in television and film, or in DVA awareness campaigns: can you think of examples which challenge the public story?
- Why are LGB and/or T+ people more likely to seek counselling for DVA rather than approaching the police or specialist DVA services? Think about the barriers to accessing these services, and how these may vary for different groups of LGB and/or T+ people.
- A number of different 'relationships services' are not usually involved in multi-agency DVA forums. What would be the value of including some of these practitioners, such as youth workers or organisations that deliver

relationship counselling? What training might they need to be part of a wider response to LGB and/or T+ DVA?

Notes

[1] We use the term LGB and/or T+ to avoid conflating sexuality and gender identity, recognising that transgender people may identify as heterosexual or LGB+. The addition of '+' signifies the inclusion of other non-normative sexualities and gender identities such as queer, pansexual, non-binary or gender-fluid.

[2] The term cisgender (or cis) describes individuals whose gender identity corresponds with their biological sex.

[3] Specialist DVA services are usually voluntary sector services which have a specific remit for victims/survivors and/or perpetrators of DVA, for example, Women's Aid agencies.

[4] We place 'abusive' in inverted commas to acknowledge that not all behaviours reported by participants were conducted with abusive intent. Closer examination of context, motives and impacts is needed to understand how power is operating in intimate relationships, as we argue in Donovan and Barnes (2020a).

[5] All participant names are pseudonyms.

References

Badenes-Ribera, L., Bonilla-Campos, A., Frias-Navarro, D., Pons-Salvador, G. and Monterde-i-Bort, H. (2016) Intimate partner violence in self-identified lesbians: a systematic review of its prevalence and correlates, *Trauma, Violence, & Abuse*, 17(3), 284–97.

Balsam, K. (2001) Nowhere to hide: lesbian battering, homophobia, and minority stress, in Kaschak, E. (ed.) *Intimate Betrayal: Domestic Violence in Lesbian Relationships*, New York, NY: Haworth Press, pp 25–37.

Barnes, R. and Donovan, C. (2016) Developing interventions for abusive partners in lesbian, gay, bisexual and/or transgender relationships, in Hilder, S. and Bettinson, V. (eds.) *Domestic Violence: Interdisciplinary Perspectives on Protection, Prevention and Intervention*, Basingstoke: Palgrave Macmillan, pp 297–320.

Barnes, R., Gunby, D., Johnson, K. and Ayres, T. (2021) Improving the mental health outcomes of Nottingham's LGBT+ populations, [online]. Available from: www2.le.ac.uk/departments/criminology/documents/improving-the-mental-health-outcomes-of-nottinghams-lgbt-populat ion-final-report-11-jan-2021 [Accessed: 15 September 2021].

Curtice, J., Clery, E., Perry, J., Phillips M. and Rahim, N. (eds.) (2019) *British Social Attitudes: The 36th Report*, London: The National Centre for Social Research.

Donovan, C. (2013) Redefining domestic violence and abuse: unintended consequences of risk assessment, in Kearney, J. and Donovan, C. (eds.) *Constructing Risky Identities in Policy and Practice*, Basingstoke: Palgrave Macmillan, pp 109–26.

Donovan, C. and Barnes, R. (2019) Making sense of discourses of sameness and difference in agency responses to abusive LGB and/or T partners, *Sexualities*, 22(5/6), 785–802.

Donovan, C. and Barnes, R. (2020a) *Queering Narratives of Domestic Violence and Abuse*, Basingstoke: Palgrave Macmillan.

Donovan, C. and Barnes, R. (2020b) Help-seeking among lesbian, gay, bisexual and/or transgender victims/survivors of domestic violence and abuse: the impacts of cisgendered heteronormativity and invisibility, *Journal of Sociology*, 56(4), 554–70.

Donovan, C. and Butterby, K. (2020) An eight day working week: LGBT+ domestic abuse sector snapshot, [online]. Available from: www.durham.ac.uk/media/durham-university/research-/research-centres/research-into-violence-and-abuse-centre-for/pdf-files/lgbtdvaorgssnapshotofaworkingweek.pdf [Accessed: 3 June 2021].

Donovan, C. and Hester, M. (2010) 'I hate the word "victim"': an exploration of recognition of domestic violence in same sex relationships, *Social Policy and Society*, 9(2), 279–89.

Donovan, C. and Hester, M. (2014) *Domestic Violence and Sexuality: What's Love Got to Do with It?*, Bristol: Policy Press.

Donovan, C., Barnes, R. and Nixon, C. (2014) The Coral Project: exploring abusive behaviours in lesbian, gay, bisexual and/or transgender relationships: interim report, [online]. Available from: www2.le.ac.uk/departments/criminology/documents/coral-project-interim-report [Accessed: 3 June 2021].

Finneran, C. and Stephenson, R. (2013) Intimate partner violence among men who have sex with men: a systematic review, *Trauma, Violence, & Abuse*, 14(2), 168–85.

Frankland, A. and Brown, J. (2014) Coercive control in same-sex intimate partner violence, *Journal of Family Violence*, 29(1), 15–22.

Hansen, M. (1993) Feminism and family therapy: a review of feminist critiques of approaches to family violence, in Hansen, M. and Harway, M. (eds.) *Battering and Family Therapy: A Feminist Perspective*, London: Sage, pp 69–81.

Hattendorf, J. (1997) Domestic violence: counseling strategies that minimize the impact of secondary victimization, *Perspectives in Psychiatric Care*, 33(1), 14–23.

Head, S. and Milton, M. (2014) Filling the silence: exploring the bisexual experience of intimate partner abuse, *Journal of Bisexuality*, 14(2), 277–99.

Hodes, C. and Mennicke, A. (2019) Is it conflict or abuse? A practice note for furthering differential assessment and response, *Clinical Social Work Journal*, 47, 176–84.

Home Office (2016) *Ending Violence against Women and Girls: Strategy 2016–2020*, London: HM Government.

Johnson, M.P. (2006) Conflict and control: gender symmetry and asymmetry in domestic violence, *Violence against Women*, 12(11), 1003–18.

McDermott, E. (2011) The world *some* have won: sexuality, class and inequality, *Sexualities*, 14(1), 63–78.

Messinger, A.M. (2011) Invisible victims: same-sex IPV in the National Violence Against Women Survey, *Journal of Interpersonal Violence*, 26(11), 2228–43.

Office for National Statistics (ONS) (2018) Women most at risk of experiencing partner abuse in England and Wales: years ending March 2015 to 2017, [online]. Available from: www.ons.gov.uk/peoplepopulationandco mmunity/crimeandjustice/articles/womenmostatriskofexperiencingpa rtnerabuseinenglandandwales/yearsendingmarch2015to2017 [Accessed: 3 June 2021].

Pence, E.L. and Shephard, M.F. (1999) An introduction: developing a coordinated community response, in Shephard, M.F. and Pence, E.L. (eds.) *Coordinating Community Responses to Domestic Violence: Lessons from Duluth and Beyond*, London: Sage, pp 3–25.

Radford, L. and Gill, A. (2006) Losing the plot? Researching community safety partnership work against domestic violence, *Howard Journal of Criminal Justice*, 45(4), 369–87.

Renzetti, C.M. (1992) *Violent Betrayal: Partner Abuse in Lesbian Relationships*, London: Sage.

Ristock, J.L. (2002) *No More Secrets: Violence in Lesbian Relationships*, Abingdon: Routledge.

Robinson, A.L. and Payton, J.L. (2016) Independent advocacy and multi-agency responses to domestic violence, in Hilder, S. and Bettinson, V. (eds.) *Domestic Violence: Interdisciplinary Perspectives on Protection, Prevention and Intervention*, Basingstoke: Palgrave Macmillan, pp 249–71.

Rogers, M. (2021) Exploring the domestic abuse narratives of trans and nonbinary people and the role of cisgenderism in identity abuse, misgendering, and pathologizing, *Violence against Women*, 27(12/13), 2187–207.

SafeLives (2018) *Free to Be Safe: LGBT+ People Experiencing Domestic Abuse: Spotlight Report*, Bristol: SafeLives.

Stanley, N. and Humphreys, C. (2014) Multi-agency risk assessment and management for children and families experiencing domestic violence, *Children and Youth Services Review*, 47(1), pp 78–85.

Stark, E. (2007) *Coercive Control: How Men Entrap Women in Personal Life*, Oxford: Oxford University Press.

Stonewall (2018) LGBT in Britain: home and communities, [online]. Available from: www.stonewall.org.uk/sites/default/files/lgbt_in_britain_ home_and_communities.pdf [Accessed: 15 September 2021].

Stonewall (2021) Key dates for lesbian, gay, bi and trans equality, [online]. Available from: www.stonewall.org.uk/key-dates-lesbian-gay-bi-and-trans-equality [Accessed: 15 September 2021].

Tavistock Centre (2016) Working relationally with couples where there is situational couple violence, [online]. Available from: https://tavistockre lationships.ac.uk/images/uploads/policy_use/policybriefings/Situational_ Couple_Violence_Nov_2016__FINAL.pdf [Accessed: 23 June 2021].

Tomsich, E.A., Tunstall, A.M. and Gover, A.R. (2015) Couples counseling and domestic violence, in Jennings, W.G. (ed.) *The Encyclopedia of Crime and Punishment*, Oxford: Wiley-Blackwell.

Trute, B. (1998) Going beyond gender-specific treatments in wife battering: pro-feminist couple and family therapy, *Aggression & Violent Behavior*, 3(1), 1–15.

Weeks, J. (2007) *The World We Have Won*, London: Routledge.

Wendt, S., Buchanan, F., Dolman, C. and Moss, D. (2020) Engagement: narrative ways of working with men when domestic violence is noticed in couple counselling, *Journal of Social Work*, 20(2), 234–56.

6

"Throwing the first punch before I got hurt": the experiences of imprisoned women who have perpetrated intimate partner violence and abuse

Jenny Mackay

Introduction

Understanding of intimate partner violence and abuse (IPVA) has steadily grown over recent decades, with public bodies across the globe now arguing that IPVA is a serious public health issue (NICE, 2014; CDC, 2020; WHO, 2021). Crime survey data in England and Wales show that in the year 2019–20, an estimated 2.1 per cent of men (513,000) and 4.9 per cent of women (1.195 million) had experienced non-sexual partner abuse (ONS, 2020a). This means that two in three victims of partner abuse are women, whereas one in three are men, with the majority of both women and men reporting the perpetrator to be of the opposite sex (ONS, 2020b). When incidents are reported and prosecuted in courts, of those convicted of an IPVA-related offence, 55,486 were men and 4,599 were women (in the year 2018–19; CPS, 2020). In the UK IPVA is not an offence in itself, as incidents are covered under existing criminal law, for example, assault or threats to kill. As such, there is no central collation of, for example, numbers of those serving prison sentences for IPVA-related offences. Thus, it is difficult to know just how many individuals are situated within the criminal justice system (CJS). Research on IPVA beyond prevalence data has focused on impact and consequences (Lagdon, Armour and Stringer, 2014; Sanz-Barbero, Barón and Vives-Cases, 2019), risk factors for perpetration (for example, Capaldi et al, 2012; Costa et al, 2015; Mackay et al, 2018) and interventions for both victims and perpetrators (for example, Stephens-Lewis et al, 2019; Trabold et al, 2020).

The plethora of research in the field has led to a narrative of IPVA that centres on a strong, domineering male perpetrator who is physically abusive to a female victim. However, more recently, there has been a burgeoning interest in male victims of IPVA as perpetrated by women, for example, exploring prevalence of victims (Nowinski and Bowen, 2012), impacts of IPVA on men (Hine, Bates and Wallace, 2020), barriers to accessing services (Wallace et al, 2019) and the demographic characteristics of male victims attending specialist support services (Hine et al, 2022). Indeed, qualitative research has highlighted substantial physical, psychological and sexual abuse perpetrated by women against men, with devastating consequences for the victims (Bates, 2020a; Hine, Bates and Wallace, 2020; Bates and Weare, 2020). Men have also reported experiencing female-perpetrated abusive behaviours such as controlling their freedoms, manipulation, isolation, gaslighting, humiliation, fear and uncertainty (Bates, 2020b). Further, since the 1980s there has been growing examination of IPVA perpetrated within female same-sex relationships, with more understanding now of prevalence, nature of the abuse and the impact of sexual minority stress (Badenes-Ribera and Bonilla-Campos, 2021). This demonstrates that the 'narrative' must include an understanding of women's perpetration of IPVA.

Perhaps at a more cautious rate, researchers are now therefore trying to understand women's perpetration of IPVA, especially since reviews exploring rates of perpetration have demonstrated notably high rates of physical, emotional and psychological violence and abuse perpetration by women (for example, Williams, Ghandour and Kub, 2008; Esquivel-Santoveña and Dixon, 2012). Further, there is an increase in women coming to the attention of the CJS as a result of perpetrating such behaviours; in England and Wales convictions increased sixfold between the years 2004 (806 convictions) and 2020 (4,948 convictions) (CPS, 2020). When men are convicted of an IPVA-related offence, this behaviour is clearly targeted by CJS practitioners as a need that must be addressed, for example, through targeted offending behaviour work (Walton et al, 2017). However, this is not automatically the case for women, and it remains unclear as to whether the needs of this group of women are being unmet.

Traditionally, women's perpetration of IPVA has been considered as self-defence, with women's use of violence in relationships taken less seriously than men's (Johnson, 2011). Some researchers have concluded that men do not perceive fear from women in relationships (Swan and Snow, 2002) and that men's use of violence in relationships exerts different, and worse, impacts to that perpetrated by women (Stark, 2006). Indeed, Stark (2010, p 208) states that women use violence 'to create an environment in which they enjoy the same autonomy, liberty and dignity they could increasingly command in school, work and in the political world'. Given that qualitative research has highlighted the serious and negative impacts of female-perpetrated IPVA on male victims (for instance, Bates, 2020a), there is a need to understand and prevent such behaviour, rather than disregard women's violence as less problematic than men's. While systematic reviews have identified that women's use of IPVA is, at times, motivated by self-defence (Bair-Merritt et al, 2010; Mackay et al, 2018), other motivations have also been established, for example, expression or management of negative feelings, control or coercion and retaliation (Mackay et al, 2018). Thus, if women's use of IPVA is only ever considered self-defence or not having a serious impact, there is a growing number of women in contact with the CJS whose needs and risks in relation to this behaviour may be ignored.

Although there is a paucity of research exploring women's perpetration of IPVA, there has been some attempt to understand what factors contribute to this phenomenon. Studies have found that for women situated within the CJS, there have been correlational associations found between IPVA perpetration and experiencing child abuse, substance use, borderline personality traits, attachment issues and experiencing trauma (see Mackay et al, 2018 for a review). However, studies have so far failed to explain the mechanisms behind these factors, that is, *why* and *how* they contribute to women resorting to using violence and/or abuse within relationships. These studies are also unable to explain the temporality of these factors; for example, it cannot be concluded whether substance use is a trigger for IPVA perpetration, a consequence of IPVA perpetration or an ongoing health problem that distally influences IPVA perpetration. Thus, this research was conducted to explore the life histories and risk markers of women who perpetrated IPVA, to further understand mechanisms underlying IPVA perpetration.

Methods

This qualitative research was granted ethical approval from the host institution and Her Majesty's Prison and Probation Service (HMPPS) National Research Committee. Contact was then made with psychology departments within prison establishments where it had been agreed the research could take place, and who agreed to host the research and the interviews. The researcher had experience of working in a prison, and therefore was able to draw keys and had full access to prison databases in order to identify and recruit participants. Given the sensitive nature of the research topic, participants' wellbeing was considered foremost in the recruitment process. Identified participants were initially invited for a consent meeting, where the research was fully explained through discussion and opportunity for questions; it was made very clear that their participation or not in the research had no bearing on their current sentence plan, in order that they felt no pressure to participate. During interviews, women's upset was handled sensitively and with careful consideration of ongoing support. Where needed, and with consent, wider prison staff were made aware that an individual had become upset and possibly needed ongoing support. Full and thorough debriefs were conducted with the women, which included conversation around positive aspects of the women's lives in order to end the interviews on a pleasant note. It was incredibly important to the researcher to ensure women felt no obligation to participate, that they were listened carefully to and supported through such a sensitive topic.

Fifteen imprisoned women aged 20–49 took part in semi-structured, life history interviews, with an aim to understand their pathways to IPVA perpetration. Simultaneously, 14 imprisoned men were interviewed with the same aim, as part of a wider study.[1] All participants were either serving a current sentence for an offence related to IPVA, or had previously been convicted of an IPVA-related offence. Interestingly, it was difficult to identify women who had been convicted of such an offence, as this was not as readily recorded as it had been with the men. Eligible women were therefore identified by reading through each woman's case files (who were serving a sentence in the two establishments where the research took place) to determine if their offences were related to IPVA, resulting in 15 women participants who agreed to participate. Eleven of the 15 women described perpetrating a complex pattern of abusive or violent behaviours against partners. A further two women stated they had only ever perpetrated a singular act of IPVA against a male partner in their lifetime (corroborated by case file data); however, both incidents were serious enough to result in death. One other described two incidents of IPVA perpetration, and a fourth woman said in her consent interview that she had been adjudicated within the prison for perpetrating IPVA against a current partner (another woman in prison) but no other information about these incidents was described or captured (she was interviewed on one occasion only). Most incidents described by participants were physical in nature. Five women identified that they were engaged in regular bidirectional violence, describing this as being with a partner in which they both frequently fought with each other. For these women, it was rarely clear who was the primary perpetrator.

Interview length ranged from one hour 12 minutes to three hours 32 minutes, with most interviews taking place across two occasions. Three women did not attend for a second interview for reasons related to pressures they were experiencing in the prison, and not related to the research. Thematic analysis (TA) was conducted on the interview data once transcribed. Themes were developed around predisposing factors (early-life factors within childhood/adolescence and emerging adulthood), precipitating factors (the immediate triggers to IPV perpetration) and perpetuating factors (the ongoing factors that maintained the problems in the women's lives).

Findings

The themes presented here represent the history of trauma and instability present in the women's lives and the motivations or triggers for perpetration of IPVA that were linked to a need to take back control and an anticipation of being hurt in relationships. These triggers are discussed in relation to how ongoing trauma and continued difficulties in interpersonal relationships perpetuated the perpetration of IPVA in the women's lives. Participants were given pseudonyms to protect their identities.

Distal factors – trauma and instability

The women had experienced various types of traumatic events, including direct interpersonal abuse and indirect experience of violence. Traumatic events were either isolated but significant, or trauma was sustained or repeatedly experienced. The most significant type of trauma experienced was abuse, most of which was sexual, but the women had also experienced trauma indirectly through witnessing violence in the family home, or the death of someone close to them. Experiencing trauma in the early years is considered an ACE (Felitti et al, 1998) and has been linked to impairment across a range of domains of a young person's development including attachment, biology, affect regulation, dissociation, behavioural control, cognition and self-concept (Cook et al, 2005).

For the most part, child sexual abuse had been perpetrated by someone the women knew; further, one woman was raped during a racially motivated attack, and two women had been victims of child sexual exploitation and were raped repeatedly by strangers. An example of this was described by Siobhan: "I could feel a weight on top of me, behind me, and on top of me, I was asleep on the sofa, so I was trying to say get off, get off, but he was sat, he was telling me shut up and he had his hand over me" (Siobhan). The women articulated deep sadness about these incidents, either through crying or talking very quietly. Jackie made a connection between her past and her current life circumstances: "I think, I wanna tell you because I think that's maybe how things have gotten to where they are." Child sexual abuse has also been found in quantitative research to be associated with perpetration of IPVA by women (Trabold et al, 2015; Rode et al, 2015). Thus, when working with women who have perpetrated IPVA, there is clearly a need to consider whether and how they have been impacted by abuse of this nature. Knowing that child sexual abuse can have a myriad of impacts on individuals (Malloy, Sutherland and Cauffman, 2021) means that this is an important aspect to consider in any intervention offer.

Physical abuse, emotional abuse and neglect were also experienced, all perpetrated by family members. As children, around half of the women were removed from their family home by social services because of abuse suffered. Familial responses to a child's trauma experiences can impact on whether a child develops complex trauma responses. Lack of support and parental emotional functioning has been linked to development of PTSD symptoms

(Cook et al, 2005). The abuse suffered by the women in this current research was reported to have been perpetrated by family members, or women said they were not believed. This was exemplified by Cathy who said she was raped by her brother and "I used to tell my mum, and they just, they ignored me and everything, 'oh you're just making it up'". Thus, the development of a complex trauma response for women who have experienced abuse in this context is understandable.

Many women also reported violence and/or abuse in the home or experienced the death of someone close to them (parents or extended family members). Specific details of violence were sometimes remembered:

'My dad pulling my mum's hair and punching her, and there was violence, I remember my dad picking up a bottle and hitting my mum in the face with it. Literally like, her jaw was hanging. ... She's got, erm, an eye fracture to the skull. And I remember my little brother going to crawl under his bed and he ripped his pants, I remember that.' (Leah)

Chloe, at age 8, was forced to watch her mother self-harm and said she vividly remembered this:

'One time she did, yeah, she, it were like, I kind of knew, there was a few times she'd lock herself in the bedroom and I'd know what she was doing, erm, like I'm not stupid even at that age, I knew what she was doing. But there was one time when, I'd gone in the room, and she was like, "well if you wanna see it that bad, like, if you wanna see it that bad, you can stay, you're not going anywhere".' (Chloe)

Many of the women spoke of *instability through abandonment*, where there was precarity and an unstable nature of their early lives across one or more domains, including home, school and family, perceived as abandonment and absence of others. This seemed to breed a feeling of the women being unable to trust others, particularly in relation to whether they would be hurt. Instability in accommodation and in family relationships are highlighted in Dunst's (1993) list of potential factors that may have an impact on child development. Early life characterised by instability and chaos meant participants had little they could rely or depend on. As a result, during adolescence, many women engaged in what might be described as 'antisocial' behaviour, for example: "We was doing burglaries ... and we was causing trouble for my mum and that, like, for erm, round the neighbourhood like" (Lacey).

Instability also made it difficult for the women to build on positive areas of their lives, as they potentially did not have the time or mental energy to focus on key developmental tasks in their life, for example, learning, building relationships or taking up common childhood hobbies/pastimes.

Instability in relationships largely related to parents or other caregivers; some women also talked about difficulties in relationships with siblings or others at school. There was a notable absence of parental or caregiver involvement in women's lives, with a particular sense of being let down when the mothers were perceived as absent, compared with a sense akin to 'acceptance' of absent fathers. It has been argued that women are expected to be nurturing and emotionally present in their role as mothers (Erikson, 2005; Parks and Barta, 2018), thus this may explain why the women in the current research expressed these feelings towards their absent mothers; women often talked about their mothers having "let them down", or not protecting them from abuse that they had experienced. For example, Leah stated that she blamed her mum when she was the victim of a serious sexual assault at the age of 4: "I love my mum, but I hated her for so long. I blamed her. And I know, it wasn't her fault ... she let me down" (Leah).

Instability was also evidenced by participants' mothers being physically absent or emotionally unavailable, leading to a sense of insecurity. For example, Sally talked about her mother escaping a violent relationship from Sally's father; while she was able to stay with her mother, the separation led to Sally's mother gaining a new "lease of life", resulting in her being largely absent in Sally's life. Jackie also discussed her mother not paying much attention to her because of a new boyfriend: "My mum was so wrapped up in him, that she never really paid attention to how I was and what I thought. So, that caused arguments between me and my mum." Emotional unavailability of parents has been associated with children's psychological difficulties (Sturge-Apple, Davies and Cummings, 2006), demonstrating the ways in which this element of instability may be a risk factor for women's future IPVA perpetration. In other ways, the emotional unavailability of a mother figure was seen in the children feeling responsible for managing their mother and her needs:

'We wouldn't mention my dad in front of my mum cos all she did was cry. We didn't want to upset her. She couldn't help it, but we didn't want to upset her and ... [sighs] I suppose my brother took over as man of the house. He was only three years older [than Susan], so, he was, it was just before his 10th birthday. So, it was just horrible. We just used to creep around, and you know, pretend nothing had happened.' (Susan)

Women also discussed instability related to relationships with their fathers. This was either related to their father's use of violence, or a lack of relationship with them. For example, for Chloe this related to violence:

'I'd be going to school and I'd have big bruises, I had big bruises round my neck and on my ... my dad used to have a habit of grabbing me by my hair and putting his hand round my throat, and then he'd like slam me into the wall, so I'd always have like a bruise down my back.' (Chloe)

When women talked about their father's absence, this usually followed parental separation. Parental absence adds to instability within the family and has been linked to later problems with adjustment (Adam, 2004). Some women had not seen their father for years:

'My real dad had fucked off by then ... I was 6, I think. Cos, he asked us what sweeties we wanted from the shop, and we never saw him again ... I remember what I asked for, a fudge. Yeah, I asked for a fudge and he just fucked off.' (Lydia)

It should be noted that there were some participants who remember distinct times in their childhood when they were getting on well with parents and would describe positive relationships at these times. These times occurred less often than the negative experiences and it seems that the overriding impact on the women stems from the negative experiences. Four women who were formally placed with foster carers all described positive relationships with these caregivers. Positive relationships between young people and their foster parents have been explained by higher parental monitoring (Cooley et al, 2021), balanced and responsive parenting styles (Wilson et al, 2003; Chamberlain et al, 2006) and by foster parents being adaptive to their foster children's needs (Brown, 2008). Given that the women in the current study often described these elements as missing from their relationships with their parents, these qualities may be able to explain the positive foster parent relationships.

Instability in relationships with siblings was related to separations that were unanticipated or related to traumatic experiences. For example, some participants were separated from their siblings when either they or their sibling were removed from the family home. Leah talked about this with regard to her older brothers, saying: "One was adopted at birth and my nan and grandad had the other one." For others, the relationship itself with the sibling was traumatic, in that it linked to the abuse experienced in their childhood/adolescence: "Erm. My older sister, the next sister above me, erm, did some naughty things to me ... erm, my mum and dad had fucked off for the summer holidays and left me with my sister [almost crying]" (Chloe).

Some described sometimes being ostracised in school, through being bullied or feeling that they were different to the other pupils:

'I didn't really find it easy to make friends, all the way through school and, erm, I got picked on by teachers which were my elders as well as people that were younger than me. So, erm, I did struggle a bit in school, there was no one to really turn to, like I had no teachers to turn to, I didn't have any help or support.' (Grace)

'Yeah, I just, do you know what, I just don't, I struggled to fit in when I was younger. I really did.' (Lydia)

This could be a reflection of 'peer rejection', a notion that has been identified as a 'chronically stressful experience' for children and adolescents (Dodge et al, 2003, p 2). There is a negative association between how well accepted children are by their peers and loneliness, and chronic loneliness has been associated with maladjustment later in life (for example, depression and problematic alcohol use; Asher and Paquette, 2003). Further, peer rejection exacerbates antisocial development in those children who are already inclined towards aggressive behaviour (Dodge et al, 2003, p 15), suggesting a possible link for the women in this sample between their problems dealing with anger in childhood and how well they were accepted by their peers. This sense of not fitting in meant that the women struggled to describe connections with others in their lives, adding to a sense of instability. These early relationships, or lack of, that the women experienced meant they were not exposed to healthy, stable relationships where they could rely upon others and be relied upon.

When women discussed the types of discipline they received while growing up (especially in adolescence), this consisted of: particularly harsh or strict discipline, inconsistent discipline between parents/caregivers or an absence of discipline and/or guidance (that is, parental monitoring). This again all contributed to instability. Parental monitoring incorporates those behaviours employed by parents that track what a child does and where they are, and has been shown to be associated with adolescent antisocial behaviour (Dishion and McMahon, 1998). Further, poor child-rearing practices in general have been found to be indirectly associated with an increased risk of IPVA perpetration via adolescent antisocial behaviour (Lussier, Farrington and Moffitt, 2009). Although this finding relates to males, the link between poor parental supervision and adolescent antisocial behaviour has been found to hold for both females and males (Stattin and Kerr, 2000). For the women interviewed, the discipline received reinforced the feeling of instability for them as it gave a sense that their caregivers, people expected to be nurturing, supportive and offering guidance, were unpredictable or unloving towards them. This was reflected in the reflections on the discipline received in childhood:

'This is the thing, I was never disciplined or anything like, I don't know, well to be fair, she did used to hit me like, and stuff, with her shoe and things like that, it didn't bother me, I didn't care like, what you gonna do, like sort of thing.' (Stephanie)

'They weren't, er, we used to get, erm, a slap. I never took a beating or anything like that. That was, erm, the humiliation side, when we got a bit older, and my mum was like, you're still not too old to go over your dad's knee. It's my step-dad, yeah that like, I think that was more the humiliation part of it.' (Lydia)

The instabilities and trauma in the women's early lives demonstrate their exposure to multiple adversities (inconsistent and harsh discipline, repeated relocations, disruption at school and abuse) and early interpersonal difficulties. The impact of adversity on a range of health and wellbeing outcomes is well documented (for instance, Davidson, Bunting and Webb, 2012). The women in this study went on to experience difficulties in managing their emotions, having mental health problems and difficulties in interpersonal relationships. It is not surprising, therefore, that the described early instability and trauma had a longer-term significant impact on them, nor that violence and/or abuse had some utilisation for them within relationships. Hence, for women situated within the CJS who have a history of perpetrating IPVA, it is vital to understand any trauma and/or instability they have experienced in order to provide appropriate support or interventions.

Triggers to IPVA perpetration – 'anticipating violence' and 'taking back control'

The women described wanting to *take back control* in their relationships by 'sticking up' for themselves and refusing to be treated badly or with disrespect. The way in which women talked about this gave the sense that the function of the violence was to prevent being treated like they have in the past and that they were now 'taking a stand'. The women felt that violence was the main way of achieving their goal of not being treated badly. This was especially linked to the varying types of ongoing trauma the women experienced, in particular IPVA victimisation. Sally exemplified this by repeatedly saying that she refused to put up with violence from men anymore, yet admitted that she was the main perpetrator of IPVA in her relationship with her husband, for example: "I've just had enough to be honest. I'm not proud of hitting him, am I heck proud of hitting him. But it was like, you're not fucking hurting me anymore, do you know what I mean?" (Sally).

Grace also made it clear that she was the more aggressive one in one particular relationship:

'Erm, basically it's because in the past I was used as a human punch bag, so therefore this is the first time that I actually stuck up for myself. And then I ended up in prison, because my friends that I was with told me, "Grace, why don't you stick up for yourself, why do you let people walk all over you?", then that kind of just played a part in my head and I'm thinking yeah, I actually am letting people walk all over me. So, therefore I stuck up for myself, got myself in prison.' (Grace)

Sometimes, the women talked about taking a stand in the context of them being hit first and then hitting back. Importantly, these were not occasions where the women used violence in order to defend themselves, but where they felt justified in using violence against their partners to make a point about not being willing to be treated a certain way. For example:

'He'd been treated like shit basically and the thing was, that was how he treated women. But I wouldn't have that, so that's what led into, escalated and went into violence. If he hit me, you were getting fucking hit back. Do you know what I mean? Simple as that.' (Lydia)

'In my life, through my life of drinking, everything in my head, my friends used to tell me every time I was drunk I'd go, "you haven't had a life like me, youse haven't been raped, youse haven't been abused", and that's what kept me drinking and drinking and drinking and if a guy went to hit me, I'd think, fucking hell, me last boyfriend did that, I'm not putting up with this shit.' (Sally)

Some women described *anticipating violence* from their partners and therefore they felt the need to strike the first blow. Violence was anticipated either at the time of the incident they were describing, or at some point in the future. The anticipation led the women to think they will "get in there first" with violence or aggression to prevent the possibility of being hurt again:

'Erm, and then started calling me all sorts of names. So, I knew he was gonna hit me, I knew it was coming. ... So, I thought, fuck ya, you're not hitting me again, you're not doing it. I picked up a knife, and I went to stab him in his neck.' (Chloe)

'I was just angry all the time. It just, I weren't used to him being there and supporting me, you know what I mean, cos the man I were with before weren't like that, so ... I think this were more of me just throwing the first punch before I got hurt.' (Ruth)

There is an interesting paradox within this theme: some women expect to be hurt, but when they are, they are increasingly enraged. The women are weary of their own pain or potential pain, but they inflict this on their intimate partners. These functions of IPVA perpetration (an anticipation of violence and wanting to take back control) could be reflective of an insecure attachment style in the women and could perhaps link to their feelings of abandonment in childhood and adolescence. Attachment anxiety, characterised by worry regarding the availability and responsiveness of one's partner and a fear of rejection and abandonment, has been found to be associated with IPVA perpetration (Gormley, 2005). Women's anticipation of being hurt and a need to take back control may be related to a fear of being rejected by their partners. It could also be a perception that their partners are unresponsive and therefore treating them badly, which may be an accurate depiction of their partner's behaviour or may be a misinterpretation. The women's developmental pathways to this point suggest the development of insecure attachments, with the sense of instability through abandonment and isolation that they reported experiencing as predisposing factors.

Ongoing trauma and difficulties: perpetuating factors

The previously mentioned descriptions of distal and proximal factors of early trauma experiences and instability had profound impacts on the women's outlook on life and relationships. These early experiences bred a sense of mistrust in others, possibly leading to the belief that the women felt a need to use violence/abuse in relationships because they anticipated violence and wanted to take back control. What seemed to be key for the perpetration of IPVA in adulthood were the ongoing difficulties and challenges that the women faced, notably problematic relationships and ongoing experiences of trauma. These perpetuating factors then acted as a sort of 'feedback loop' to those immediate triggers to IPVA perpetration, maintaining the risk that women would be violent and/or abusive.

The women were often entrenched in unhealthy cycles of behaviour within relationships and struggled to deal with stresses placed upon those relationships. In their interviews, the women shared beliefs about their relationships and about violence that justified and perpetuated using violence against partners. These types of attitudes were suggested by Bandura (1999; 2002) as examples of how individuals morally disengage from causing harm to others. For example, this was seen in attitudes such as their partner deserved what happened to them, as discussed by Chloe: "Cos she deserved it, all the times she got mouthy to me and said all these horrible things to me". Further, violence occurred where the women held attitudes about their male partners as weak, thus linking to dominant notions of masculinity, for example: "Because he was so soft on me, that's why I pull at his strings more and more ... he's very, for a man, he's weak, yeah. I know that sounds horrible to say" (Jackie).

'I felt more in control because like I was always asking him to get me a drink and he'd get me a drink. I'd ask him to get me something and he'd get me something. So, therefore, I became my ex, I, and he became the weaker one.' (Grace)

Women continued to experience trauma in their adult lives (often sustained, and often in relation to IPVA victimisation), and this resulted in severe consequences for them. Three women were victims of IPVA in same-sex relationships and 11 victims in heterosexual relationships. Examples of some of the extreme abuse women received included being locked in houses/ sheds, being fed dog food, not being allowed a phone, being kicked in the face with steel-toe-capped boots and daily beatings. These experiences sometimes resulted in hospital admissions due to extremely serious injuries. Women described difficulties in living with the fact that this had happened to them, and again, these ongoing traumatic experiences seemed to maintain the problems women experienced and thus maintain the risk of them perpetrating IPVA. In fact, many of the proximal triggers to IPVA perpetration linked to them being a victim of IPVA, for example, their perceptions about relationships and about violence. Further, the women's IPVA victimisation maintained a sense of isolation, of being different and of experiencing instability and chaos in their lives. IPVA victimisation and its impact for women is widely documented, with negative implications for women's physical health, mental health and quality of life (Pico-Alfonso et al, 2006; Dillon et al, 2013; Hegarty et al, 2013), and this was certainly seen in this sample.

Conclusion and recommendations

The findings in this chapter highlight the importance of understanding not only women's developmental histories, but the motivations behind and triggers to IPVA perpetration. Women discussed impacts of *trauma* and *instability* in their early lives and ongoing *difficulties within interpersonal relationships* and *trauma experiences*. They also discussed being motivated by a need to *take back control* and an *anticipation of being hurt* in relationships. The experiences presented demonstrate the distressing narratives of women who have perpetrated IPVA. A complex history of trauma and instability contributed to them becoming vulnerable to anticipating violence in relationships. Further, the women believed that their only option was to use violence/abuse, which was, at times, severe and devastating. Their troubling and disturbing experiences were incredibly difficult to hear, and it was obvious that they had left their marks on the women who took part in this study. While it was the case that some women used violence in self-defence at times, they also discussed using violence as a way to take back control and/or to prevent violence that they were (rightly or wrongly) anticipating. That the women demonstrated this need to take back control may be a more unexpected finding from this research, as control is often discussed in relation to male perpetrators. This work has therefore demonstrated how vital it is to understand the ongoing traumatic experiences that the women were exposed to, and the ways in which this perpetuated the problems in the women's lives. This then has implications for how women can be supported in their journey to desistance from IPVA perpetration, taking into account the factors that will improve quality of life and aid desistance. The work has also highlighted how crucial it is to fully understand the function of an individual's use of violence or abuse, rather than applying a 'broad brush' explanation for a behaviour, so as not to miss a potential clinical need that may be addressed in interventions.

Findings from this research suggest that theoretical explanations for IPVA perpetration must take into account concepts related to: the impact of complex trauma responses; ongoing trauma experienced, interpersonal relationship dynamics and problems; ongoing mental health difficulties; and the function of IPVA behaviours. Theory should then drive interventions offered to women who are convicted of IPVA-related offences. When women enter the CJS in England and Wales today, professionals are encouraged to work with them in a trauma-informed way (MoJ, 2018). This would seem to be particularly important for this group of women, who have used violence and/or abuse in intimate relationships, as their stories show just how much trauma and instability they have been exposed to.

As a result of this research, it is suggested that there are several components that should be considered when designing and developing interventions for IPVA perpetrators. Before any intervention, there should be an in-depth approach to assessment (ideally through a case formulation approach) in order to gain a thorough understanding of an individual's history and IPVA perpetration. Any work that perpetrators undertake should be trauma-informed and strengths-based and should have a strong focus on interpersonal skills and emotion management, perhaps through a Dialectical Behaviour Therapy (DBT) approach. It is also key that individuals are supported to develop positive identities, to reduce the sense of isolation and the problematic relationships in their lives. Importantly, while interventions or work may need to be gender-sensitive, these suggestions apply to all individuals, no matter their gender; the importance of understanding the individual, their story and their need, no matter what they have done, cannot be underestimated if we wish to improve people's lives and reduce the chances that they will perpetrate violence/abuse in their relationships again.

Reflection points

- What else can CJS practitioners do to respond more effectively to IPVA perpetration by women?

- How can practitioners ensure they are sensitive to the enduring impact of trauma, but empower and support women not to turn to violence within their intimate relationships?
- Would you respond to women and men differently if they admitted that they had been violent/abusive to an intimate partner? Why do you think you would respond in this way? Do you think we should respond differently?

Note

[1] The wider study refers to doctoral research conducted by the author, in which both imprisoned women and men were interviewed to explore a comparison of their treatment needs in relation to IPVA perpetration (see Mackay, 2020).

References

Adam, E.K. (2004) Beyond quality: parental and residential stability and children's adjustment, *Current Directions in Psychological Science*, 13(5), 210–13.

Asher, S.R. and Paquette, J.A. (2003) Loneliness and peer relations in childhood, *Current Directions in Psychological Science*, 12(3), 75–8.

Badenes-Ribera, L. and Bonilla-Campos, A. (2021) Domestic violence and abuse within female same-sex relationships, in Devaney, J., Bradbury-Jones, C., Macy, R.J., Overlien, C. and Holt, S. (eds.) *The Routledge International Handbook of Domestic Violence and Abuse*, Oxon: Routledge, pp 267–82.

Bair-Merritt, M.H., Shea Crowne, S., Thompson, D.A., Sibinga, E., Trent, M. and Campbell, J. (2010) Why do women use intimate partner violence? A systematic review of women's motivations, *Trauma, Violence, & Abuse*, 11(4), 178–89.

Bandura, A. (1999) Moral disengagement in the perpetration of inhumanities, *Personality and Social Psychology Review*, 3(3), pp 193–209.

Bandura, A. (2002) Selective moral disengagement in the exercise of moral agency, *Journal of Moral Education*, 31(2), 101–19.

Bates, E.A. (2020a) 'No one would ever believe me': an exploration of the impact of intimate partner violence victimization on men, *Psychology of Men & Masculinities*, 21(4), 497.

Bates, E.A. (2020b) 'Walking on egg shells': a qualitative examination of men's experiences of intimate partner violence, *Psychology of Men & Masculinities*, 21(1), 13–24.

Bates, E.A. and Weare, S. (2020) Sexual violence as a form of abuse in men's experiences of female-perpetrated intimate partner violence, *Journal of Contemporary Criminal Justice*, 36(4), 582–95.

Brown, J.D. (2008) Foster parents' perceptions of factors needed for successful foster placements, *Journal of Child and Family Studies*, 17, 538–54.

Capaldi, D.M., Knoble, N.B., Shortt, J.W. and Kim, H.K. (2012) A systematic review of risk factors for intimate partner violence, *Partner Abuse*, 3(2), 231–80.

CDC (2020) Intimate partner violence, [online]. Available from: www.cdc. gov/violenceprevention/intimatepartnerviolence/index.html [Accessed: 18 June 2021].

Chamberlain, P., Price, J.M., Reid, J.B., Landsverk, J., Fisher, P.A. and Stoolmiller, M. (2006) Who disrupts from placement in foster and kinship care?, *Child Abuse and Neglect*, 30, 409–24.

Cook, A., Spinazzola, J., Ford, J., Lanktree, C., Blaustein, M., Cloitre, M. et al (2005) Complex trauma in children and adolescents, *Psychiatric Annals*, 35(5), 390–8.

Cooley, M.E., Thompson, H.M., Wojciak, A.S. and Mihalec-Adkins, B.P. (2021) Parental monitoring by foster parents, youth behaviours and the youth–foster parent relationship, *Child & Family Social Work*, 1, 1–13.

Costa, B.M., Kaestle, C.E., Walker, A., Curtis, A., Day, A., Toumbourou, J.W. and Miller, P. (2015) Longitudinal predictors of domestic violence perpetration and victimization: a systematic review, *Aggression and Violent Behavior*, 24, 261–72.

CPS (2020) VAWG annual data tables, [online]. Available from: www.cps. gov.uk/sites/default/files/documents/publications/VAWG-Annual-Data-Tables-Year-Ending-March-2020.xlsx [Accessed: 18 June 2021].

Davidson, G., Bunting, L. and Webb, M.A. (2012) *Families Experiencing Multiple Adversities: A Review of the International Literature*, Belfast: Barnardo's Northern Ireland.

Dillon, G., Hussain, R., Loxton, D. and Rahman, S. (2013) Mental and physical health and intimate partner violence against women: a review of the literature, *International Journal of Family Medicine*, 313909, doi:9/2013/1155.10/org.doi.dx://h.

Dishion, T.J. and McMahon, R.J. (1998) Parental monitoring and the prevention of child and adolescent problem behavior: a conceptual and empirical formulation, *Clinical Child and Family Psychology Review*, 1(1), 61–75.

Dodge, K.A., Lansford, J.E., Burks, V.S., Bates, J.E., Pettit, G.S., Fontaine, R. et al (2003) Peer rejection and social information-processing factors in the development of aggressive behavior problems in children, *Child Development*, 74(2), 374–93.

Dunst, C.J. (1993) Implications of risk and opportunity factors for assessment and intervention practices, *Topics in Early Childhood Special Education*, 13(2), 143–53.

Erikson, R.J. (2005) Why emotion work matters: sex, gender and the division of household labor, *Journal of Marriage and Family*, 67(2), 337–51.

Esquivel-Santoveña, E.E. and Dixon, L. (2012) Investigating the true rate of physical intimate partner violence: a review of nationally representative surveys, *Aggression and Violent Behavior*, 17(3), 208–19.

Felitti, V.J., Anda, R.F., Nordenberg, D., Williamson, D.F., Spitz, A.M., Edwards, V. et al (1998) Relationship of childhood abuse and household dysfunction to many of the leading causes of death in adults: the adverse childhood experiences (ACE) study, *American Journal of Preventive Medicine*, 14(4), 245–58.

Gormley, B. (2005) An adult attachment theoretical perspective of gender symmetry in intimate partner violence, *Sex Roles*, 52(11–12), 785–95.

Hegarty, K.L., O'Doherty, L.J., Chondros, P., Valpied, J., Taft, A.J., Astbury, J. et al (2013) Effect of type and severity of intimate partner violence on women's health and service use: findings from a primary care trial of women afraid of their partners, *Journal of Interpersonal Violence*, 28(2), 273–94.

Hine, B., Bates, E.A. and Wallace, S. (2020) 'I have guys call me and say "I can't be the victim of domestic abuse"': exploring the experiences of telephone support providers for male victims of domestic violence and abuse, *Journal of Interpersonal Violence*, 37(7–8), NP5594–NP5625, doi:10.1177/0886260520944551.

Hine, B., Bates, E.A., Mackay, J. and Graham-Kevan, N. (2022) Comparing the demographic characteristics, and reported abuse type, contexts and outcomes of help-seeking heterosexual male and female victims of domestic violence: Part I – who presents to specialist services? *Partner Abuse*, 13(1), doi:10.1891/PA-2021-0009.

Johnson, M.P. (2011) Gender and types of intimate partner violence: a response to an anti-feminist literature review, *Aggression and Violent Behavior*, 16(4), 289–96.

Lagdon, S., Armour, C. and Stringer, S. (2014) Adult experience of mental health outcomes as a result of intimate partner violence victimisation: a systematic review, *European Journal of Psychotraumatology*, 5(1), 1–12.

Lussier, P., Farrington, D.P. and Moffitt, T.E. (2009) Is the antisocial child father of the abusive man? A 40-year prospective longitudinal study on the developmental antecedents of intimate partner violence, *Criminology*, 47(3), 741–80.

Mackay, J. (2020) *Comparing the Treatment Needs of Women and Men Who Perpetrate Intimate Partner Violence and Abuse*, Unpublished PhD thesis, Coventry: Coventry University.

Mackay, J., Bowen, E., Walker, K. and O'Doherty, L. (2018) Risk factors for female perpetrators of intimate partner violence within criminal justice settings: a systematic review, *Aggression and Violent Behavior*, 41, 128–46.

Malloy, L., Sutherland, J. and Cauffman, E. (2021) Sexual abuse disclosure among incarcerated female adolescents and young adults, *Child Abuse & Neglect*, 116(1), 104147, doi:10.1016/j.chiabu.2019.104147.

Ministry of Justice (MoJ) (2018) Female Offender Strategy, [online] June. Available from: https://assets.publishing.service.gov.uk/government/uplo ads/system/uploads/attachment_data/file/719819/female-offender-strat egy.pdf [Accessed: 15 April 2021].

NICE (2014) Domestic violence and abuse: multi-agency working, [online] 26 February. Available from: www.nice.org.uk/guidance/PH50 [Accessed: 15 April 2021].

Nowinski, S.N. and Bowen, E. (2012) Partner violence against heterosexual and gay men: prevalence and correlates, *Aggression and Violent Behavior*, 17(1), 36–52.

ONS (2020a) Domestic abuse victim characteristics, England and Wales: year ending March 2020, [online] 25 November. Available from: www. ons.gov.uk/peoplepopulationandcommunity/crimeandjustice/articles/ domesticabusevictimcharacteristicsenglandandwales/yearendingmarch2 020#toc [Accessed: 1 September 2021].

ONS (2020b) Partner abuse in detail, England and Wales: year ending March 2018, [online] 25 November. Available from: www.ons.gov.uk/ peoplepopulationandcommunity/crimeandjustice/articles/partnerabuse indetailenglandandwales/yearendingmarch2018#more-about-domestic-abuse [Accessed: 1 September 2021].

Parks, E.S. and Barta, K. (2018) Are you my mother? Perpetuating gender inequality through listening: expectations and relational roles, *Journal of Research in Gender Studies*, 8(1), 28–48.

Pico-Alfonso, M.A., Echeburúa, E. and Martinez, M. (2008) Personality disorder symptoms in women as a result of chronic intimate male partner violence, *Journal of Family Violence*, 23(7), 577–88.

Rode, D., Rode, M. and Januszek, M. (2015) Psychosocial characteristics of men and women as perpetrators of domestic violence, *Polish Psychological Bulletin*, 46(1), 53–64.

Sanz-Barbero, B., Barón, N. and Vives-Cases, C. (2019) Prevalence, associated factors and health impact of intimate partner violence against women in different life stages, *PLoS ONE*, 14(10), e0221049, doi:10.1371/ journal.pone.0221049.

Stark, E. (2006) Commentary on Johnson's 'Conflict and control: gender symmetry and asymmetry in domestic violence', *Violence against Women*, 12(11), 1019–25.

Stark, E. (2010) Do violent acts equal abuse? Resolving the gender parity/ asymmetry dilemma, *Sex Roles*, 62(3), 201–11.

Stattin, H. and Kerr, M. (2000) Parental monitoring: a reinterpretation, *Child Development*, 71(4), 1072–85.

Stephens-Lewis, D., Johnson, A., Huntley, A., Gilchrist, E., McMurran, M., Henderson, J. et al (2019) Interventions to reduce intimate partner violence perpetration by men who use substances: a systematic review and meta-analysis of efficacy, *Trauma, Violence, & Abuse*, 22(5), 1262–1278, doi:10.1177/1524838019882357.

Sturge-Apple, M.L., Davies, P.T. and Cummings, E.M (2006) Impact of hostility and withdrawal in interparental conflict on parental emotional unavailability and children's adjustment difficulties, *Child Development*, 77(6), 1623–41.

Swan, S.C. and Snow, D.L. (2002) A typology of women's use of violence in intimate relationships, *Violence Against Women*, 8(3), 286–319.

Trabold, N., McMahon, J., Alsobrooks, S., Whitney, S. and Mittal, M. (2020) A systematic review of intimate partner violence interventions: state of the field and implications for practitioners, *Trauma, Violence, & Abuse*, 21(2), 311–25.

Trabold, N., Swogger, M.T., Walsh, Z. and Cerulli, C. (2015) Childhood sexual abuse and the perpetration of violence: the moderating role of gender, *Journal of Aggression, Maltreatment & Trauma*, 24(4), 381–99.

Wallace, S., Wallace, C., Kenkre, J., Brayford, J. and Borja, S. (2019) Men who experience domestic abuse: a service perspective, *Journal of Aggression, Conflict and Peace Research*, 11(2), 127–37.

Walton, J., Ramsay, L., Cunningham, C. and Henfrey, S. (2017) New directions: integrating a biopsychosocial approach in the design and delivery of programs for high risk service users in Her Majesty's Prison and Probation Service, *Advancing Corrections: Journal of the International Corrections and Prison Association*, 3, 21–47.

WHO (2021) Violence against women, [online]. Available from: www.who.int/news-room/fact-sheets/detail/violence-against-women [Accessed: 15 April 2021].

Williams, J.R., Ghandour, R.M. and Kub, J.E. (2008) Female perpetration of violence in heterosexual intimate relationships: adolescence through adulthood, *Trauma, Violence, & Abuse*, 9(4), 227–49.

Wilson, K., Petrie, S. and Sinclair, I. (2003) A kind of loving: a model of effective foster care, *British Journal of Social Work*, 33, 991–1003.

7

"It feels like a mini victory": alternative routes to justice in experiences of online misogyny

Jo Smith

Introduction

Online misogyny is an umbrella term, encompassing a range of behaviours occurring on the internet which demonstrate a 'dislike of, contempt for, or ingrained prejudice against women' (Lexico, 2021). This includes the non-consensual sharing of indecent images, or 'revenge porn' (Citron and Franks, 2014; McGlynn and Rackley, 2017; McGlynn, Rackley and Houghton, 2017), the receipt of graphic images, or 'dickpics' (Vitis and Gilmour, 2017; Tweten, 2018), cyber-stalking (Citron, 2014) and various forms of harassment (Henry and Powell, 2016; Powell and Henry, 2017; Smith, 2019). Although online abuse is not new (see, for example, Dibbell, 1993; Herring, 1999), the scale, form and reach of such abuse has expanded (Amnesty International, 2017; Vogels, 2021) as the internet has become a greater part of our everyday lives (Office for National Statistics [ONS], 2021). In some cases the abuse that targets women focuses solely on gender, but it is also clear that online misogyny intersects with other characteristics including race (Madden et al, 2018), religion (Easat-Daas, 2021; Klaff, 2021), gender identity (Colliver, 2021; Rogers, 2021) and disability (Healy, 2021).

This chapter explores a specific facet of online misogyny: online gendered hate. This term describes those acts of aggression, abuse and threatening words or behaviours which target women in online public spaces (Smith, 2019). The acts can be verbal or written, in the form of comments on social media sites, videos on YouTube or TikTok and/or can be image-based (Sarkeesian, 2014; 2015; Mantilla, 2015). It has been argued that women can experience this form of abuse directly or indirectly (Smith, 2019). Direct abuse is that which targets a particular woman and is received by them from the perpetrator (Smith, 2019), with many examples of this specific targeting evident in academic work, news articles and on social media sites (Lewis, 2011; Sarkeesian, 2014; Mantilla, 2015; Amnesty International, 2017; Line, 2017; Rawlinson, 2018; Hunt, 2019; Borowiec, 2021). Indirect abuse occurs when a woman is not herself the target of abuse, but encounters other women being subject to abuse in online spaces (Smith, 2019). This may be through reading articles or blogs about online abuse, or by these indirect recipients actually encountering other women receiving abusive messages in online spaces.

A developing body of literature has begun to explore the consequences of online gendered hate. A consistent theme in the literature is that online gendered hate is harmful in 'embodied, tangible and real' ways (Powell and Henry, 2017, p 50). Harms can be experienced to an individual's mental and physical wellbeing (Penny, 2011; Mantilla, 2015; Barlow and Awan, 2016; Adams, 2018), and financial and professional life (Adams, 2018; Jane, 2018). There are also notable effects on women's sense of safety online, and comfort in engaging in online spaces or online discussions (Mantilla, 2015; Smith, 2019). These acts of misogynistic abuse have led women to feel constrained and controlled in their participation, resulting in women retreating from particular conversations, activities or spaces online (Herring, 1999; Herring et al, 2002; Citron, 2014; Jane, 2014; 2017b; Vitak et al, 2017; Veletsianos et al, 2018).

The idea of women being controlled and constrained by acts of male violence is nothing new: it has long been argued among feminist scholars (see, for example, Millet, 1970; Griffin, 1971; Brownmiller, 1975) that domestic abuse, sexual violence and the myriad of other forms of violence against women are manifestations of the power that men hold within patriarchy to oppress and control women. Mehrhof and Kearon (1971, p 80), for example, see gender-based violence as 'a political act of *oppression* (never rebellion) exercised by members of a powerful class on members of the powerless class' (original emphasis). In some senses online misogynistic abuse is simply 'old wine' (of patriarchy and male power) in 'new bottles' (of the internet); it is another way in which women's behaviours and engagement are controlled and restrained. The patriarchy which privileges men's voices and silences those which try to challenge and shatter these problematic power structures pervade our online spaces as much as they do in our offline world.

Jane (2017b, pp 50–1) has created a taxonomy of responses to online gendered hate, separated into 'flight' and 'fight'. Flight describes those acts of self-silencing, censoring one's behaviour or removing oneself from the abusive or risky situations by attempting to avoid the abuse and any subsequent harms. This in turn results in the 'chilling effect' of restricting women's engagement in online spaces (Jane, 2017b, p 58), silencing women's voices and driving women from public spaces (Smith, 2019). Fight behaviours, on the other hand, are strategies which defy, subvert, challenge and engage in activism to contend with online gendered hate (Jane, 2017b, p 51). The first of the four fight responses, 'one-on-one engagement with attackers' (Jane, 2017b, p 51), involves a recipient of abuse confronting the perpetrator about their behaviours in ways which may be abusive, humorous or reasoned. The other three fight responses are described by Jane as 'activism'. Traditional activism includes raising awareness of online misogyny (such as through campaigns, petitions, lobbying and speaking out about abuse) and providing support to other targets of abuse. Performance activism sees women using their creativity to respond to online abuse, for example, turning abuse into comedy skits (Clever Pie and Isabel Fay, 2012; Mic, 2014; Mash Report, 2018), artwork (Jenkins, n.d.; Roth, 2014) or songs (Guttfull, 2017). The final form of fight activism is digital vigilantism or 'digilantism', acts which involve 'any combination of trickery, persuasion, reputation assaults, surveillance, public shaming, calls to action, and so on' (Jane, 2017a, p 3). This can involve identity theft, denial-of-service (DoS) attacks,[1] scamming and, perhaps more commonly in relation to misogynistic abuse, the public outing of abusers by individuals and groups (Jane, 2016). These fight acts might respond to individual acts of misogyny or can involve more general attempts to challenge a culture of online misogyny and seek to reclaim online space for women's voices.

Significantly, fight responses present an important alternative to formal routes to justice, such as seeking involvement of the police or reporting to the social media sites, which have left women dissatisfied and without remedy. Pavan (2017, p 67), for example, noted that social media sites fail to deal with abuse within their borders, creating spaces which reinforce 'discriminatory and abusive behaviours towards women'. Others have presented experiences of engagement with law enforcement as unsatisfactory, frustrating and often futile (Mantilla, 2015; Lewis, Rowe and Wiper, 2016; Smith, 2019). Legislative provisions[2] in England and Wales are outdated, or present problems when it comes to prosecuting online gendered hate,[3] and guidance on the prosecution of online social media offences is clear that comments which are merely shocking, rude, offensive or 'banter' are unlikely to reach the threshold for prosecution (Crown Prosecution Service [CPS], 2018). Here, the current lack of recognition of misogyny as a strand of hate crime stymies attempts to use the law to address online gendered hate. Where a social media offence involves a 'protected characteristic',[4] specific consideration must be given to prosecution to ensure that hate crimes are prosecuted 'fairly, firmly and robustly' (CPS, 2018). The exclusion of gender as a protected characteristic means there is no obligation to deal with online misogyny in a fair, firm and robust way.

The Online Safety Bill 2021, described as a 'milestone in the Government's fight to make the internet safe', proposes measures to 'protect children online and tackle some of the worst abuses on social media, including racist hate crimes' (Gov.uk, 2021). This Bill includes measures to require websites to remove illegal and harmful content, the creation of statutory codes of practice and greater powers given to Ofcom to issue warnings, fines and court orders to enforce compliance by online service providers. How far the measures in this Bill will address gender-based hate will become more apparent if and when the Bill is brought into law, guidance on its application is created and the provisions are put into practice.

This chapter focuses on how women who are receiving online abuse – directly or indirectly – respond to this with attempts to resist or fight back against it. Drawing on data from a wider project (Smith, 2019) looking at feminist women's experiences of online gendered hate, an account will be given showing how women engage in fight responses (Jane, 2017b). After a brief explanation of the research methods, the chapter will focus on three of Jane's taxonomical categories – engagement with perpetrators of abuse, traditional activism and digilantism. This is followed by a broader discussion of fight strategies as an alternative approach to dealing with online gendered hate, drawing links with other literature. The chapter concludes by asking the reader to consider the risks and rewards of alternative routes to justice following online misogynistic abuse, and the role that the criminal justice system (CJS) and social media sites ought to play in responding to and policing online abuse. It raises questions about the role and requirements of legislation to better monitor and manage these harmful acts.

Methods

According to Cook and Fanow (1985), feminist research is situated on five core tenets: centring gender within the research; acknowledging consciousness raising and activism; appreciation of the importance of ethics and the risk of exploiting participants; challenging the axiomatic assumption of the importance of objectivity; and accentuating how research can empower women and transform lives. These principles were woven throughout the research, which used online focus groups and interviews to gather women's experiences of online gendered hate.

Women were recruited for this research using adverts in women and non-binary only social media spaces, snowball sampling and targeted emails to those who had been the recipients of online gendered hate.[5] Participants were sought based on specific criteria: aged over 18, based in England and Wales, identifying as a woman and as a feminist or feminist sympathising. Two groups of women were created from these recruitment techniques. The first comprised of six women who self-identified as direct recipients of online misogyny and who participated in one-to-one online interviews. The second group comprised of 20 women who had encountered online misogyny indirectly, who participated in focus groups and then follow-up interviews. Two of the 'indirect' participants did not partake in the subsequent interviews, and one undertook the interview but did not wish to be part of a focus group. Analytical engagement with the data occurred throughout collection, transcription and reflective practices. Data was then coded and analysed thematically (Dey, 1993; Braun and Clarke, 2012; Saldana and Leavy, 2014) using the software MaxQDA. More information about the research methods can be found in Smith (2019).

Throughout the research careful attention was given to ethics, keeping in mind guidance provided by the British Society of Criminology (2015) and the Association of Internet Researchers (Markham and Buchanan, 2012), alongside the feminist principles I brought to this research. Women taking part in the research were invited to use a pseudonym or their own name within the study, in recognition of the importance of allowing women silenced online to speak about their experiences with their own voices. This also challenged the paternalistic assumption that anonymisation of participants is the best and most ethically sound approach (Giordano et al, 2007; Guenther, 2009). Informed consent was obtained from all women who took part in the research, and care was taken to avoid using third-party data (such as the names of those perpetrating online gendered hate) unless this data was publicly available and analysed independently of the original source (for example, taken from other academic sources, rather than directly from social media). While it felt somewhat vexing to take such care over those who had perpetrated abuse, the deplorability of their actions was not justification to use their (albeit public) words without consent in this research engaged in three of Jane's (2017b, pp 50–1) fight responses: engagement with the perpetrators of abuse, traditional activism and digilantism. One of the women who took part in the research had used 'performance activism', the fourth of Jane's (2017b) fight responses, in producing creative writing about her experiences. However, her discussions of this were limited and so it was hard to draw conclusions from her experiences. The absence of this 'performance activism' strategy from the data may reflect that this approach may only occur to those already engaged in performance as part of their career or as a hobby; those who do not already write, draw, craft and so on may not think to incorporate their experiences into this. There are also risks that such pieces draw attention to the abuse being experienced, and despite positive attention through discussion of and the sharing of the performances, they may also draw in those seeking to perpetrate online gendered hate. The other strategies, while also having the potential to create both positive and negative attention, were more widely adopted. It is also important to note that while Jane (2017b) created these distinct categories of response, she is clear that there is overlap in the ways in which these manifest, as is apparent in the data from this research. So, for example, blogging about one's experiences of abuse can be a form of traditional activism (recording and publicly discussion online gendered hate) but could also amount to performance and, if involving naming and shaming perpetrators, digital vigilantism.

Addressing the perpetrators of online misogyny

One approach to fighting back against online gendered hate came through engagement with those who were perpetrating abuse, a strategy that could benefit the recipients of abuse, but which also carried risks. Anna M. found that by engaging publicly with those who were targeting her for abuse, she could defuse their anger, correct misassumptions and allow her views to be better understood:

> 'It was quite common that people would start off quite "grrr", quite angsty ... and I'd kind of engage, within the confines of 140 characters ... it was astonishing how often people would say "thank you very much for engaging. I still disagree with you". ... To me it felt like it vindicated me for my stance of not just blocking people for being abusive. There were limits but at the same time I think there was something really suboptimal in that you couldn't really tell the difference between what kind of person they were until you'd done a bit of engaging with them.' (Anna M.)

Through her engagement with those targeting her, Anna M. could attempt to understand and then address why the abuse was occurring. In opening up, rather than closing down, discussions, she was able to create a space where her views were better understood and where the discussion could be pacified. While beneficial for Anna M., this strategy was less successful for another woman who received abuse, Claire H., who found that engagement with those who were targeting her led to continuation and amplification of the abuse. For both women, assessing the likely outcome of this engagement was difficult: neither woman knew who was targeting them, or (before engaging with them) why, and so they could not easily predict the efficacy of this approach. This highlights the risks involved with this strategy, including that engagement would amplify awareness of the abuse a woman had already received and inspire others to join in and 'dogpile'[6] the target. Why some women might receive a positive response to engagement with the perpetrators of abuse, and others become targeted further, is not known. However, Anna M. was targeted for more persistent but less 'serious' abuse on a range of matters related to her job, whereas Claire H. had experienced a huge amount of abuse, including dogpiling and incitement to further abuse, in response to a single incident. Those targeting Anna M. may have been more open to discussion about what she was saying because it was part of an ongoing dialogue about her views and her work; as a result, engagement may have been a more productive approach for her.

It was not only those who received abuse directly who engaged with perpetrators of online gendered hate: some of the women who indirectly received abuse also undertook this form of fight response, something which again carried risks and rewards. Wanting to create a distraction from the target of abuse, and thus give them some respite, motivated Gillian L. to try to shift attention from the recipient of abuse to herself; in Gillian L.'s words, to draw "their fire by turning Sauron's eye away from the hobbits towards myself".[7] Engagement by those indirectly involved could also be a way that the women who took part in the research could support those women being subjected to abuse. Juliet K. noted that "it's about looking after the person being abused, which may or may not mean calling the abuser out" where doing so "feels like it might not be a total lost cause". Indirect recipients of abuse therefore saw reward in helping and supporting another woman online. There is also symbolic value in such interventions, with engagement by bystanders demonstrating overt disapproval of the acts. This might send a message to the perpetrator, and to others observing, that these abusive missives are unacceptable and that women would not stand by silently and accept them. It is a form of resistance to the 'appropriate' ways of doing difference (Perry, 2001) by defying expectations of women as passive victims.

Nevertheless, engagement with abuse was also risky for those indirectly experiencing online gendered hate. These women had not (yet) been targeted, and by intervening they risked receiving specific abuse themselves. This dissuaded some women: "I'd like to think that I would [intervene], but I don't know if I would to be honest ... I'd be too scared of being targeted myself" (Sasha T.). For both direct and indirect recipients of online gendered hate, there were benefits and risks to this fight strategy. The risks of responding might be higher for the direct recipients of abuse as they are already within sight of the "eye of Sauron" (to use Gillian L.'s analogy), and the experience of receiving abuse was a 'known' to them. However, they had some strategies in place for coping with the harms, and might be able to assess at least some of the risks and benefits of engagement. Such strategies were varied and included: handing over social media accounts to trusted friends; staying with friends or family to avoid the risk of and minimise the fear of offline violence; avoiding comments threads on their social media accounts; self-imposed restrictions on engaging with the internet at particular times (such as in the evenings or before bed); using exercise to 'work out' some of the stress and anxiety generated by receiving abuse; changing passwords and adding further security to online accounts; and leaving specific online spaces for periods of time. Experiencing online abuse gave those women with direct experience the knowledge of what worked for them in helping them to cope; faced with further abuse, they could put these strategies into action to minimise the risk of harm. Those who had only encountered abuse indirectly were perhaps less likely to have the abuse turned on them, placing them at a lower risk if they engaged, but they had no knowledge of how being targeted might affect them, or how they could deal with this.

While they might speculate about how they would cope, they lacked the experience to know if this would work.

Resisting online gendered hate through 'traditional' activism

Traditional activism, in Jane's taxonomy (2017b, p 51), involves raising awareness of online abuse and its consequences, advocacy, recording and publicly discussing online gendered hate, campaigning and providing support for other women. One form of activism undertaken by Kate S. was the recording of the abuse she received in a blog. This documented what she was being subjected to and raised awareness of the quantity and quality of the online gendered hate. While a form of traditional activism, this was also indirect engagement with the perpetrators of abuse, and of digilantism: naming and shaming abusers in public. Furthermore, it served as something of a 'flight' response – by "just us[ing] my phone to screenshot screenshot screenshot screenshot screenshot and then I just go on to the blog and just 'up up up up up up up'", Kate S. did not have to deal with reading the abuse, but could maintain a record should this ever be needed. It also allowed her to maintain a degree of vigilance over the online gendered hate she received (Smith, 2019, p 168).

Particularly evident in the data as a form of traditional activism was how the women in this research sought and provided support networks for each other, even if only via informal conversations. Anna M., who had been the target of abuse, had considered what she would have wanted as support, and had developed a strategy of making positive posts on the feeds of targets of abuse. Not only was this easy, but it was safe as "it's not conflict ... the perpetrators might not even see it". Anna M. went on to comment that

> 'if you send them [the target] a nice picture of a kitten or a flower or a mountain or you know a sunset, in amongst all of their stream of crap they've then got some nice solidarity of someone going "this is to brighten your day" and it's something which is really easy to do.' (Anna M.)

Another traditional activist approach can be seen in the use of online feminist spaces by women in this research. For some, this involved seeking support, reassurance and help from other members. These communities, often with exclusively women and non-binary membership, gave women a safe place in which to discuss their experiences or their views on 'controversial' topics,[8] and to practise arguments that they wished to make in more public online forums. Cath B. noted that

> 'online space, especially safer spaces that are locked down to women only, and the people that identify away from the gender binary, those

are spaces where you can test out your discussions, you work on ideas so if someone actually says "not all men" to me in a post, how can I respond to this with a good argument? And I think that's brilliant, I think the internet has given spaces for people new to feminism to really ... practise their feminism.' (Cath B.)

While these online communities were safe places to which women could flee and avoid abuse, they were also spaces of learning and engagement for all members of the community. For those receiving abuse, using these groups raised awareness of what was happening, while others in the community could provide support to those being subject to online hate. Notable was that members of the community worked collaboratively to create arguments and provide evidence to help their members engage in challenging and risky discussions on social media sites. This was apparent in Sophia C.'s experience: through seeking help from her feminist online spaces, she had developed confidence in speaking out online, in building up and evidencing the arguments she wanted to make. She was then able to engage in public debate and also challenge those acting abusively. There is something quite emotive about this combination of consciousness raising and collective action which sees women creating discussion and ideas together as a community, to be taken back into online public spaces. Furthermore, this community-centric approach recalls feminist praxis and activism seen within offline feminist spaces since second-wave feminism.

DIY justice through digilantism

Women who participated in this research did not often engage in digilantism themselves, but celebrated such acts undertaken by other women, particularly trolling,[9] dogpiling and being abusive towards the perpetrators. In the focus group extract following, the women were discussing seeing the targets of online misogyny engaging in digilante acts by those targets perpetrating abuse against their abusers:

Cath B.:   I guess the men doing the dogpiling see it as the same thing.
Elle B.:   I don't think so, because the power balance isn't the same.
Jill H.:   It often gets called the same – but as Elle said the power balance is very different.
Elle B.:   Plus it's usually debate/rebuttal coming from us, but men pile on with threats/insults.
Cath B.:   I think, when women wade in, we're supporting each other, showing that we're not lone voices. That the woman isn't alone, that we want our voices to be heard.

Elle B.:   We're always trying to get them to understand. They're trying
            to get us to be quiet.

When targeted in the form of dogpiling, Elle B. experienced this as
abuse – she had commented that: "I criticised [edited name] who described
[edited name] as being mad and I said I was really uncomfortable with him
doing that, and he tweeted that to his five billion followers who just, it
immediately became a dogpile". As a response to abuse, however, she saw
this as educational, about trying to claim space online, as acts of consciousness
raising and support of other women. These behaviours, which amounted to
abuse when targeting women, were subverted to be understood as acts of
resistance and defiance, lauded because they showed the powerless fighting
back against the powerful.

Interestingly, the women in this research drew a distinction between the
use of abusive behaviours (such as dogpiling and trolling) as a form of online
gendered hate by the perpetrators of online misogyny, and the use of these
same behaviours by the targets of online abuse as digilante acts of resistance
and fighting back. There was therefore a difference in the 'quality' of the
act, depending on who was using them: the former being abuse, and the
latter being resistance and defiance. This distinction in the interpretation of
abusive acts can be framed within an understanding of abusive behaviours
as the previously mentioned manifestations of power. Online gendered
hate can be understood as a form of hate crime (Smith, 2019) in which the
acts are a 'mechanism of power and oppression, intended to reaffirm the
precarious hierarchies that characterise a given social order' (Perry, 2001,
p 10). Thus, the dogpiling, or threats or any number of other forms of online
abuse are acts of power and oppression, designed to maintain male power
and patriarchal social order.

Although the perpetrators of online gendered hate are not always men (see,
for example, Lewis, 2014), this does not preclude acts of online gendered
hate perpetrated by women as being manifestations of power. Firstly, the
ways in which power can intersect along different identity characteristics
can situate women who experience privilege because of *some* of their
identities, for example, race, as oppressors. Furthermore, we can understand
acts of violence against women perpetrated by other women as upholding
patriarchy and male power, through, for example, internalised misogyny
(Szmanski, Gupta and Carr, 2009). However, when acts of abusive behaviour
are undertaken as digilantism by those lower in the social hierarchies against
their oppressors, these acts are qualitatively different. They lack the power
that makes the acts forms of abuse, because the women engaging in the
acts lack the power to 'place them on a par with those perpetrating online
gendered hate' (Smith, 2019, p 216).

The women in this research also noted digilante acts could feel cathartic, with Sasha T. stating: "I like those stories where you know, they find out their girlfriends' phone number or something and talk to them, it feels like a mini victory." There was a sense that these acts were doing *something* to challenge online gendered hate. This stands in stark contrast to the experiences of reporting to the police or social media sites, where women felt that reporting was futile. Only one woman (Kate S.) reported the abuse she had received to the police, describing this process as "really unpleasant". She saw little point in going to the police about online abuse, saying there had been "about 40 or 50 other ones that I've reported that they've done nothing about". Other women who had received abuse perceived that nothing would be done and so saw little point in engaging with the CJS:

> 'There is so much abuse that goes on online I guess I just sort of thought to myself, "is anything going to be done about this, probably not" ... and I think the only way it would have been done is if it did escalate to offline, so if those people did come to my work and did harass me in the real world or did try and engage in violence in the real world.' (Charlotte B.)

This ambivalence towards reporting to the police because of a perception that nothing would be done was mirrored by those women who had encountered online abuse indirectly. Although some women in this research were sympathetic to the challenges of policing the internet,[10] others felt that the police had little interest in trying to meet these challenges:

> 'What, I'm going to phone up the police and say I've seen somebody I know online has had a death threat ... generously they are overstretched and don't have the time to investigate it. Ungenerously they don't give a shit because it happens all the time because it's normal, because women receiving death threats online for talking about feminism is the normality. In a way that somebody pulling a knife on somebody in club is not.' (Sylvia P.)

Women in this research, both direct and indirect recipients of abuse, were even more sceptical of the efficacy of reporting to social media sites, with participants saying "I have reported to Facebook and found that it didn't violate community standards" (Sophia C.). The women within this research felt that the policies and practices of social media sites were abstruse and inconsistently applied, and pushed responsibility back on to the users to block abusive accounts and delete problematic content, rather than the sites themselves taking action against the abusers.

It is therefore no surprise that to these women digilantism felt like holding the perpetrators to account, and even finding some sort of justice, albeit at times verging on revenge: giving the perpetrators a (small) taste of their own medicine, and imposing punishment in the form of social sanction through disintegrative shaming[11] (Wall and Williams, 2007, pp 406–7). Nevertheless, one should not overlook that such an approach can contribute to social media spaces being toxic and abusive, with scope for 'bad actors' to use the framing of digilantism as resistance to disguise behaviour which is just abusive.

Conclusion

Developing from scepticism and negative experiences of formal routes to justice, women adopt alternative strategies to try to prevent, limit or challenge online gendered hate. Although no single approach is 'best', and indeed women in this study engaged in a variety of different strategies at different times, together, these 'fight' responses provide an opportunity to attempt to reclaim power and space online. This is particularly significant given online gendered hate acts as a manifestation of patriarchal power and control; through adopting approaches which enable women to take action, such strategies can empower women. However, while there may be benefits to such approaches, there are also risks associated with fighting back. On an individual level, it could make oneself a target, and be faced with further and more serious levels of abuse. On a broader level, these strategies can place responsibility for challenging abuse into the hands of women and/or require women to police their online spaces. In making women responsible for ensuring that they are not the victims of male violence, attention can shift away from the perpetrators of abuse (Maher, McCulloch and Fitz-Gibbon, 2017, p 22), limiting the accountability of such perpetrators for their actions. Alternative approaches to finding justice in experiences of online gendered hate can also distract from holding to account the CJS and social media sites for their failings. As Sylvia P. noted, there is a distinction in the way physical spaces and online spaces are policed:

'If I was in a nightclub and somebody came up and threatened me with a knife and a bouncer saw them, then they would be out of that club on their arse really quickly. Because the nightclub doesn't want to get a reputation of allowing that sort of violence on their premises. And if they do allow that violence on their premises and they don't do anything about it, then they could be held liable, particularly if it was an employee for failing to protect those people because they have a duty of care to them in their space. I do not understand why that does not get applied online.' (Sylvia P.)

It is also important to acknowledge that the more extreme 'fight' responses, those associated with digilantism, can involve the targets of online gendered hate undertaking actions that are, at least superficially, as bad as some of the acts of the perpetrators. While it is arguable that there are qualitative differences owing to the aforementioned power dynamics, nevertheless, digital vigilantism may contribute to online spaces becoming more unpleasant.

In adopting these 'fight' strategies, women's acts challenge abuse at two levels. On a 'micro' level, women who are challenging individual acts of abuse, such as through engagement with those being abusive or digilantism, are addressing direct examples of misogyny and gendered hate from a specific individual or group. However, at a more 'macro' level, the acts of resistance also attempt to carve out spaces for women's presence and voices, challenge male dominance in social media spaces (Megarry, 2014, p 49) and push back against the given social order. These are attempts to reshape dynamics online and, in doing so, spaces of resistance can form.

This resistance can be in specific forums or communities (Herring et al, 2002; Gaden, 2007; Wazny, 2010; Drüeke and Zobl, 2016), which can provide safety and support, as noted in the findings of this research. Lewis et al (2015) noted these online spaces act as being 'safe from' abuse and 'safe to' learn and express oneself, and Clark-Parsons' (2017) study frames the safe-space Facebook group 'Girl Army' as a counterpublic space for members to support each other. Another significant site of resistance is via hashtags (Dixon, 2014; Horeck, 2014), with academic literature noting how these are valuable resources for the development of feminist counterpublics: to bring women together, to provide a 'space' for discussions about feminism, for the sharing of resources and for challenging misogyny (Shaw, 2013; Sadowski, 2016; Lopez et al, 2018). As a whole, the creation of these places of resistance can be understood within Fraser's (1990, p 67) idea of 'subaltern counterpublics' whereby places contain 'members of subordinated social groups invent and circulate counter discourses to formulate oppositional interpretations of their identities, interests and needs'.

Although Fraser's original work preceded widespread use of the internet, the internet might be seen as particularly conducive to the formation of subaltern counterpublics. This simply means that the properties of the internet and particularly social media sites are such that it is easier to find and form connections with like-minded users, enabling groups, and counterpublics, to emerge. boyd (2010, p 46), in her discussion of social networking sites as networked publics, examines how 'structural affordances' of technologies shape these networked publics. These affordances – persistence, replicability, scalability and searchability[12] – may benefit those perpetrating abuse, by allowing their acts to be disseminated, recorded or seen by a vast audience. However, they may also allow women who want to challenge misogyny and patriarchy to find each other, to share resources, to form and develop identities and interests.

A final point for consideration is to note the importance of the indirect recipients of abuse, or bystanders to online gendered hate. The research overall was interested in this group of women, with existing academic research focusing almost exclusively on those who had been directly targeted. The study found support for the idea that when one woman is targeted for abuse because of her feminist and female identity, other women online see this and modify their behaviours to avoid becoming targeted themselves. However, on a more positive note, many of the women in this study who saw abuse occurring also joined those being targeted for abuse to try to resist and challenge online misogyny. Their awareness of what was happening encouraged these indirect recipients of abuse to step forward and support the targets of abuse, to help create safer spaces for conversation, collaboration and collective action, and to take other actions to challenge online gendered hate more broadly.

In some ways it is unsurprising that women who experience online gendered hate are sceptical of engaging with the CJS. Reports of the failings in rape cases (see, for example, Barr and Topping, 2021; Her Majesty's Inspectorate of Constabulary and Fire and Rescue Services, 2021) hardly inspire confidence that the police and the CPS will take online misogynistic abuse seriously. With limited legislation criminalising online misogyny or holding social media providers to account, CPS guidance that discourages prosecution and the exclusion of gender from the recognised strands of hate crime, the law does not yet seem to take online gendered hate seriously. Whether the Online Safety Bill 2021 changes this is yet to be seen.

It is heartening then to see that women turn to alternative routes to justice. These acts of collective resistance highlight the unacceptability of online abuse, attempt to reshape some virtual spaces and remind us that online gendered hate is not a 'personal' issue to be dealt with by individuals, but a 'public' problem. With women coming together to support each other and develop opposition to online misogyny, we are presented with a powerful picture of feminist activism and praxis in the 21st century and online world.

Reflection points

- Where traditional routes to justice fail, women look to alternative strategies. While these can have benefits for individual women, feminist communities and online feminist spaces, might you consider the risks and problems associated with alternative approaches?
- How can we best address and challenge online gendered hate in ways which are effective, keep women safe from the risks of harm, and which hold perpetrators to account, without placing undue responsibility on women?

- Do alternative routes to justice reduce the accountability of the CJS and social media sites to better police themselves?

Notes

[1] 'A denial-of-service attack is characterised by an explicit attempt by attackers to prevent the legitimate use of a service. A distributed denial-of-service [DDoS] attack deploys multiple machines to attain this goal' (Mirkovic and Reiher, 2004, p 40).

[2] The two key pieces of legislation which can criminalise online gendered hate are s1 Malicious Communications Act 1988 and s127 Communications Act 2003.

[3] Bakalis (2018) presents a useful analysis of the various potential laws which could be used to prosecute online hate and the challenges that these present.

[4] Disability, race, religion, transgender identity, sexual orientation (CPS, 2017).

[5] The women who were sent targeted emails were high-profile women who had discussed their experiences of abuse in various on- and offline forums, or were women who other participants knew and suggested the researcher contact. Many of the women were identified through news articles and websites, and academic books and journal articles, in which these women's experiences were discussed.

[6] 'A situation in which criticism or abuse is directed at a person or group from multiple sources' (Oxford Dictionaries, 2019a).

[7] A reference to *Lord of the Rings* (Tolkien, 1992).

[8] The targets of online gendered hate are often those who discuss issues of feminism, politics, violence against women and other identity characteristics such as race or ethnicity. However, women have also received abuse for such 'controversial' topics as cycling, a comic book cover, a play in a basketball game and cooking (Mantilla, 2015, pp 29–30).

[9] 'A troller is a CMC [computer-mediated communication] user who constructs the identity of sincerely wishing to be part of the group in question, including professing, or conveying pseudo-sincere intentions, but whose real intention(s) is/are to cause disruption and/or to trigger or exacerbate conflict for the purposes of their own amusement' (Hardaker, 2010, p 237).

[10] Such as the police lacking the necessary resources or expertise to undertake investigations, as well as broader issues of the anonymity of perpetrators, and the question of who has responsibility for investigating an offence that occurs in the geographically borderless online world.

[11] Shaming can be reintegrative or disintegrative/stigmatising, according to Braithwaite (2000). Reintegrative approaches treat the offender as a good person who has done something bad, and as such seeks to encourage desistance from the bad behaviour through the shaming. Deintegrative shaming treats the offender as a bad person, not deserving of forgiveness or reintegration into the community.

[12] Persistence refers to the capturing, recording and archiving of what is said online. Replicability is about how technologies can enable online communications to be copied, disseminated, altered or replicated. Scalability refers to the ways in which what we say online may be visible to a vast (and often unknown) audience. Searchability looks to how online technologies make it simple for us to find people and content.

References

Adams, C. (2018) 'They go for gender first': the nature and effect of sexist abuse of female technology journalists, *Journalism Practice*, 12(7), 850–69, doi:10.1080/17512786.2017.1350115.

Amnesty International (2017) Toxic Twitter – a toxic place for women, Amnesty International, [online]. Available from: www.amnesty.org/en/latest/research/2018/03/online-violence-against-women-chapter-1/ [Accessed: 10 May 2018].

Bakalis, C. (2018) Rethinking cyberhate laws, *Information & Communications Technology Law*, 27(1), 86–110, doi:10.1080/13600834.2017.1393934.

Barlow, C. and Awan, I. (2016) 'You need to be sorted out with a knife': the attempted online silencing of women and people of Muslim faith within academia, *Social Media + Society*, 2(4), 1–11.

Barr, C. and Topping, A. (2021) CPS accused of betraying rape victims as prosecutions hit record low, *The Guardian*, [online] 22 July. Available from: www.theguardian.com/law/2021/jul/22/cps-accused-of-betraying-victims-as-prosecutions-hit-record-low [Accessed: 31 August 2021].

Borowiec, S. (2021) Hana Kimura death: man charged over cyberbullying of Japanese reality TV star, The Guardian, [online] 31 March. Available from: www.theguardian.com/world/2021/mar/31/hana-kimura-death-man-charged-over-cyberbullying-of-japanese-reality-tv-star [Accessed: 24 May 2021].

boyd, d. (2010) Social network sites as networked publics: affordances, dynamics, and implications, in Papacharissi, Z. (ed.) *Networked Self: Identity, Community, and Culture on Social Network Sites*, Abingdon: Routledge, pp 39–58, doi:10.4324/9780203876527-8.

boyd, d. (n.d.) what's in a name, danah boyd, [online]. Available from: www.danah.org/name.html [Accessed: 31 August 2021].

Braithwaite, J. (2000) Reintegrative shaming, in Paternoster, R. and Bachman, R. (eds.) *Explaining Criminals and Crime: Essays in Contemporary Criminological Theory*, Los Angeles, CA: Roxbury. Available from: http://johnbraithwaite.com/wp-content/uploads/2016/05/2000_Reintegrative-Shaming.pdf [Accessed: 31 August 2021].

Braun, V. and Clarke, V. (2012) Thematic analysis, in Cooper, H., Camic, P.M., Long, D.L., Panter, A.T., Rindskopf, D. and Sher, K.J. (eds.) *APA Handbook of Research Methods in Psychology*, Washington DC: American Psychological Association, pp 57–71.

British Society of Criminology (2015) *British Society of Criminology: Statement of Ethics*, Nottingham: British Society of Criminology. Available from: www.britsoccrim.org/new/docs/BSCEthics2015.pdf [Accessed: 18 June 2018].

Brownmiller, S. (1975) *Against Our Will: Men, Women and Rape*, New York: Simon and Schuster.

Citron, D.K. (2014) *Hate Crimes in Cyberspace*, Cambridge, MA: Harvard University Press.

Citron, D.K. and Franks, M.A. (2014) Criminalising revenge porn, *Wake Forest Law Review*, 49(2), 345–91.

Clark-Parsons, R. (2017) Building a digital girl army: the cultivation of feminist safe spaces online, *New Media & Society*, 20(4), 2125–44, doi:10.1177/1461444817731919.

Clever Pie and Isabel Fay (2012) Thank You Hater!, [online]. Available from: www.youtube.com/watch?time_continue=261&v=uz2jbCJXkpA [Accessed: 11 January 2019].

Colliver, B. (2021) 'Not the right kind of woman': transgender women's experiences of transphobic hate crime and trans-misogyny, in Smith, J. and Zempi, I. (eds.) *Misogyny as Hate Crime*, London: Routledge, pp 213–27.

Communications Act (2003) Available from: www.legislation.gov.uk/ukpga/2003/21/contents [Accessed: 17 October 2017].

Cook, J.A. and Fanow, M.M. (1985) Knowledge and women's interests: issues of epistemology and methodology in feminist sociological research, *Sociological Inquiry*, 56(1), 2–29, doi: 10.1111/j.1475-682X.1986.tb00073.x.

Crown Prosecution Service (CPS) (2017) Hate crime, Crown Prosecution Service, [online]. Available from: www.cps.gov.uk/hate-crime [Accessed: 30 October 2018].

CPS (2018) Social media: guidelines on prosecuting cases involving communications sent via social media, Crown Prosecution Service, [online] 21 August. Available from: www.cps.gov.uk/legal-guidance/social-media-guidelines-prosecuting-cases-involving-communications-sent-social-media [Accessed: 3 November 2019].

Dey, I. (1993) *Qualitative Data Analysis: A User Friendly Guide for Social Scientists*, Abingdon: Routledge.

Dibbell, J. (1993) A rape in cyberspace, [online]. Available from: www.julian dibbell.com/texts/bungle_vv.html [Accessed: 23 May 2015].

Dixon, K. (2014) Feminist online identity: analyzing the presence of hashtag feminism, *Journal of Arts and Humanities*, 3(7), 34–40.

Drüeke, R. and Zobl, E. (2016) Online feminist protest against sexism: the German-language hashtag #aufschrei, *Feminist Media Studies*, 16(1), 35–54.

Easat-Daas, A. (2021) Misogyny, hate crimes and gendered Islamophobia: Muslim women's experiences and responses, in Smith, J. and Zempi, I. (eds.) *Misogyny as Hate Crime*, London: Routledge, pp 140–54.

Fraser, N. (1990) Rethinking the public sphere: a contribution to the critique of actually existing democracy, *Social Text*, 25/26, 56–80.

Gaden, G. (2007) Carnival of feminists, *Thirdspace: A Journal of Feminist Theory & Culture*, 7(1). Available from: http://journals.sfu.ca/thirdspace/index.php/journal/article/view/resources_carnivals [Accessed: 8 April 2016].

Giordano, J., O'Reilly, M., Taylor, H. and Dogra, N. (2007) Confidentiality and autonomy: the challenge(s) of offering research participants a choice of disclosing their identity, *Qualitative Health Research*, 17(2), 264–75.

Gov.uk (2021) Landmark laws to keep children safe, stop racial hate and protect democracy online published, [online] 12 May. Available from: www.gov.uk/government/news/landmark-laws-to-keep-child ren-safe-stop-racial-hate-and-protect-democracy-online-published [Accessed: 26 August 2021].

Griffin, S. (1971) Rape: the all-American crime, *Ramparts*, 10(3), 1–8.

Guenther, K.M. (2009) The politics of names: rethinking the methodological and ethical significance of naming people, organizations, and places, *Qualitative Research*, 9(4), 411–21.

Guttfull (2017) Keyboard warrior, Guttfull bandcamp, [online]. Available from: https://guttfull.bandcamp.com/track/keyboard-warrior [Accessed: 10 October 2018].

Hardaker, C. (2010) Trolling in asynchronous computer-mediated communication: from user discussions to academic definitions, *Journal of Politeness Research*, 6(2), 215–42.

Healy, J. (2021) An exposition of sexual violence as a method of disablist hate crime, in Smith, J. and Zempi, I. (eds.) *Misogyny as Hate Crime*, London: Routledge, pp 178–94.

Henry, N. and Powell, A. (2016) Technology-facilitated sexual violence: a literature review of empirical research, *Trauma, Violence, & Abuse*, 19(2), 195–208, doi:10.1177/1524838016650189.

Her Majesty's Inspectorate of Constabulary and Fire and Rescue Services (HMICFRS) (2021) A joint thematic inspection of the police and Crown Prosecution Service's response to rape – phase one: from report to police or CPS decision to take no further action, [online]. Available from: www. justiceinspectorates.gov.uk/hmicfrs/publication-html/a-joint-thematic-ins pection-of-the-police-and-crown-prosecution-services-response-to-rape-phase-one/ [Accessed: 31 August 2021].

Herring, S.C. (1999) The rhetorical dynamics of online harassment, *The Information Society*, 15, 151–67.

Herring, S.C., Job-Sluder, K., Scheckler, R. and Barab, S. (2002) Searching for safety online: managing 'trolling' in a feminist forum, *The Information Society*, 18(5), 371–84, doi:10.1080/01972240290108186.

Horeck, T. (2014) #AskThicke: 'blurred lines', rape culture, and the feminist hashtag takeover, *Feminist Media Studies*, 14(6), 1105–7, doi:10.1080/ 14680777.2014.975450.

Hunt, E. (2019) Little Mix's Jesy Nelson on surviving the trolls: 'people were saying horrific things', *The Guardian*, [online] 8 September. Available from: www.theguardian.com/tv-and-radio/2019/sep/08/little-mixs-jesy-nelson-on-surviving-the-trolls-people-were-saying-horrific-things [Accessed: 24 May 2021].

Jane, E.A. (2014) 'Your a ugly, whorish, slut', *Feminist Media Studies*, 14(4), 531–46, doi:10.1080/14680777.2012.741073.

Jane, E.A. (2016) Online misogyny and feminist digilantism, *Continuum*, 30(3), 284–97, doi:10.1080/10304312.2016.1166560.

Jane, E.A. (2017a) Feminist digilante responses to a slut-shaming on Facebook, *Social Media + Society*, 3(2), 1–10, doi:10.1177/2056305117705996.

Jane, E.A. (2017b) Feminist flight and fight responses to gendered cyberhate, in Vitis, L. and Segrave, M. (eds.) *Gender, Technology and Violence*, Abingdon, Oxon: Routledge, pp 45–61.

Jane, E.A. (2018) Gendered cyberhate as workplace harassment and economic vandalism, *Feminist Media Studies*, 18(4), 575–91, doi:10.1080/14680777.2018.1447344.

Jenkins, C. (n.d.) Bad blood, [online]. Available from: https://casey-jenkins.com/works/bad-blood/ [Accessed: 18 October 2018].

Klaff, L. (2021) The intersection of antisemitism and misogyny, in Smith, J. and Zempi, I. (eds.) *Misogyny as Hate Crime*, London: Routledge, pp 155–77.

Lewis, H. (2011) 'You should have your tongue ripped out': the reality of sexist online abuse, New Statesman, [online] 3 November. Available from: www.newstatesman.com/blogs/helen-lewis-hasteley/2011/11/comments-rape-abuse-women [Accessed: 24 July 2015].

Lewis, H. (2014) John Nimmo and Isabella Sorley: a tale of two 'trolls', New Statesman, [online] 8 January. Available from: www.newstatesman.com/media/2014/01/john-nimmo-and-isabella-sorley-tale-two-trolls [Accessed: 7 June 2018].

Lewis, R., Sharp, E., Remnant, J. and Redpath, R. (2015) 'Safe spaces': experiences of feminist women-only space, *Sociological Research Online*, 20(4), 1–14, doi:10.5153/sro.3781.

Lewis, R., Rowe, M. and Wiper, C. (2016) Online abuse of feminists as an emerging form of violence against women and girls, *British Journal of Criminology*, azw073, 57(6), 1462–1481, doi:10.1093/bjc/azw073.

Lexico (2021) Misogyny, Oxford: Oxford University Press. Available from: www.lexico.com/definition/misogyny [Accessed: 24 May 2021].

Line, H. (2017) Diane Abbott just read out some of the shocking racist abuse she receives online, *The Independent*, [online] 12 July. Available from: www.independent.co.uk/news/uk/politics/diane-abbott-racism-speech-commons-abuse-labour-mp-a7838206.html [Accessed: 19 November 2018].

Lopez, K.J., Muldoon, M.L. and McKeown, J.K.L. (2018) One day of #Feminism: Twitter as a complex digital arena for wielding, shielding, and trolling talk on feminism, *Leisure Sciences*, 41(3), 203–220, doi:10.1080/01490400.2018.1448022.

Madden, S., Janoske, M., Briones Winkler, R., Edgar, A.N., Vickery, J.R. and Everback, T. (2018) Mediated misogynoir: intersecting race and gender in online harassment, in Vickery, J.R. and Everbach, T. (eds.) *Mediating Misogyny: Gender, Technology, and Harassment*, Cham: Springer International Publishing, pp 71–90, doi:10.1007/978-3-319-72917-6_4.

Maher, J., McCulloch, J. and Fitz-Gibbon, K. (2017) New forms of gendered surveillance? Intersections of technology and family violence, in Vitis, L. and Segrave, M. (eds.) *Technology and Violence*, Abingdon, Oxon: Routledge, pp 14–27.

Malicious Communications Act (1988) Available from: www.legislation.gov.uk/ukpga/1988/27/section/1 [Accessed: 17 October 2017].

Mantilla, K. (2015) *Gendertrolling: How Misogyny Went Viral*, Santa Barbara, CA: Praeger.

Markham, A. and Buchanan, E. (2012) Ethical decision making and internet research. Association of Internet Researchers, [online]. Available from: http://aoir.org/reports/ethics2.pdf [Accessed: 28 April 2016].

The Mash Report (2018) How not to abuse people on social media, [online]. Available from: www.facebook.com/bbctwo/videos/how-notto-abuse-people-on-social-media-the-mash-report/1904837896491339/ [Accessed: 11 January 2019].

McGlynn, C. and Rackley, E. (2017) Image-based sexual abuse, *Oxford Journal of Legal Studies*, 37(3), 534–61, doi:10.1093/ojls/gqw033.

McGlynn, C., Rackley, E. and Houghton, R. (2017) Beyond 'revenge porn': the continuum of image-based sexual abuse, *Feminist Legal Studies*, 25(1), 25–46, doi:10.1007/s10691-017-9343-2.

Megarry, J. (2014) Online incivility or sexual harassment? Conceptualising women's experiences in the digital age, *Women's Studies International Forum*, 47, 46–55, doi:10.1016/j.wsif.2014.07.012.

Mehrhof, B. and Kearon, P. (1971) Rape: an act of terror, *Notes from the Third Year*, 79–81.

Mic (2014) Feminists read mean tweets, [online]. Available from: https://youtu.be/UHC3VgsNXKg [Accessed: 10 October 2018].

Millet, K. (1970) *Sexual Politics*, New York: Doubleday.

Mirkovic, J. and Reiher, P. (2004) A taxonomy of DDoS attack and DDoS defense mechanisms, *ACM SIGCOMM Computer Communication Review*, 34(2), 39, doi:10.1145/997150.997156.

Office for National Statistics (ONS) (2021) *Internet Users, UK: 2020*, London: Office for National Statistics. Available from: www.ons.gov.uk/businessindustryandtrade/itandinternetindustry/bulletins/internetusers/2020 [Accessed: 23 April 2021].

Online Safety Bill (2021) Available from: https://assets.publishing.service.gov.uk/government/uploads/system/uploads/attachment_data/file/985033/Draft_Online_Safety_Bill_Bookmarked.pdf [Accessed: 31 August 2021].

Oxford Dictionaries (2019) Dogpile, Oxford: Oxford University Press. Available from: https://en.oxforddictionaries.com/definition/dogpile [Accessed: 10 November 2022].

Pavan, E. (2017) Internet intermediaries and gender-based violence, in Segrave, M. and Vitis, L. (eds.) *Gender, Technology and Violence*, Abingdon, Oxon: Routledge, pp 62–78.

Penny, L. (2011) A woman's opinion is the mini-skirt of the internet, *The Independent*, [online] 4 November. Available from: www.independent.co.uk/voices/commentators/laurie-penny-a-womans-opinion-is-the-mini-skirt-of-the-internet-6256946.html [Accessed: 19 November 2018].

Perry, B. (2001) *In the Name of Hate: Understanding Hate Crimes*, London: Routledge.

Powell, A. and Henry, N. (2017) *Sexual Violence in a Digital Age*, London: Palgrave Macmillan.

Rawlinson, K. (2018) Labour MP calls for end to online anonymity after '600 rape threats', *The Guardian*, [online] 11 June. Available from: www.theguardian.com/society/2018/jun/11/labour-mp-jess-phillips-calls-for-end-to-online-anonymity-after-600-threats [Accessed: 28 January 2019].

Rogers, M. (2021) Trans identities, cisgenderism and hate crime, in Smith, J. and Zempi, I. (eds.) *Misogyny as Hate Crime*, London: Routledge, pp 195–212.

Roth, A. (2014) A woman's room online, Skepchick, [online]. Available from: http://skepchick.org/2014/09/a-womans-room-online/ [Accessed: 11 January 2019].

Sadowski, H. (2016) From #aufschrei to hatr.org: digital–material entanglements in the context of German digital feminist activisms, *Feminist Media Studies*, 16(1), 55–69, doi:10.1080/14680777.2015.1093090.

Saldana, J. and Leavy, P. (2014) Coding and analysis structures, in Leavy, P. (ed.) *The Oxford Handbook of Qualitative Research*, Oxford: Oxford University Press, pp 581–605.

Sarkeesian, A. (2014) @FemFreq: I usually don't share the really scary stuff. But it's important for folks to know how bad it gets [TRIGGER WARNING], [online]. Available from: https://twitter.com/femfreq/status/504718160902492160 [Accessed: 10 November 2022].

Sarkeesian, A. (2015) One week of harassment on Twitter, Feminist Frequency, [online]. Available from: http://femfreq.tumblr.com/post/109319269825/one-week-of-harassment-on-twitter [Accessed: 2 February 2015].

Shaw, F. (2013) Still 'searching for safety online': collective strategies and discursive resistance to trolling and harassment in a feminist network, *Fibreculture Journal*, 22, 93–108.

Smith, J. (2019) *Feminist Women's Experiences of Online Gendered Hate*, Surrey: University of Surrey. Available from: http://epubs.surrey.ac.uk/852351/ [Accessed: 5 July 2021].

Szmanski, D.M., Gupta, A. and Carr, E.R. (2009) Internalised misogyny as a moderator of the link between sexist events and women's psychological distress, *Sex Roles*, 61, 101–9.

Tolkien, J.R.R. (1992) *The Lord of the Rings*, London: Grafton.

Tweten, A. (2018) *Bye Felipe: Disses, Dick Pics, and Other Delights of Modern Dating*, Philadelphia: Running Press Adult.

Veletsianos, G., Houlden, S., Hodson, J. and Gosse, C. (2018) Women scholars' experiences with online harassment and abuse: self-protection, resistance, acceptance, and self-blame, *New Media & Society*, 20(12), 4689–708, doi:10.1177/1461444818781324.

Vitak, J., Chadha, K., Steiner, L. and Ashktorab, Z. (2017) Identifying women's experiences with and strategies for mitigating negative effects of online harassment, in *Proceedings of the 2017 ACM Conference on Computer Supported Cooperative Work and Social Computing – CSCW '17. The 2017 ACM Conference*, Portland, OR: ACM Press, pp 1231–45, doi:10.1145/2998181.2998337.

Vitis, L. and Gilmour, F. (2017) Dick pics on blast: a woman's resistance to online sexual harassment using humour, art and Instagram, *Crime, Media, Culture*, 13(3), 335–55, doi:10.1177/1741659016652445.

Vogels, E.A. (2021) The state of online harassment, Pew Research Centre, [online]. Available from: www.pewresearch.org/internet/2021/01/13/the-state-of-online-harassment/ [Accessed: 24 May 2021].

Wall, D.S. and Williams, M. (2007) Policing diversity in the digital age: maintaining order in virtual communities, *Criminology & Criminal Justice*, 7(4), 391–415, doi:10.1177/1748895807082064.

Wazny, K.M. (2010) Feminist communities online: what it means to be a Jezebel, *B Sides*, 1–23. [Online]. Available from: https://pubs.lib.uiowa.edu/bsides/article/id/27890/ [Accessed: 10 November 2022].

8

The conversation isn't over: gaining justice for women and families

Isla Masson, Natalie Booth and Lucy Baldwin

Introduction

The collection of works in this second volume from the WFCJ network highlights several important and intersecting issues facing women and families experiencing punishment, abuse and (in)justice. When the WFCJ network was launched in 2018 we wanted to bring together like-minded individuals who were undertaking vital work with women and families, particularly those with personal experience of the criminal justice system (CJS). We feel strongly that these voices and experiences, if facilitated and disseminated more widely, could inform and shape positive change. The sharing of knowledge and the inclusion of conversations and debates remain key to our ongoing mission. We also believe that through collaboration and joint working, opportunities for change in policy, practice and research are more within our grasp. Together we are stronger. Recognising this potential and watching the network blossom through growing Twitter followers (@WomenFamilyCri1) and the seminar series (the latter which more recently moved online due to the ongoing pandemic) provided motivation to produce this second collection. As with the first volume, we hope that this book broadens the reach of the network to help us to achieve these commitments and acts as an important text that inspires action.

We are proud that the contributors represent different voices working in related fields, including academics, practitioners and service users, as this means that the discussions are varied and diverse. Reiterating the introduction, we felt it important to reflect on the representation of contributors hosted in the first volume – and network more widely. To that end we were delighted to be able to host chapters which reflect important, intersectional work that includes gender, sexuality, ethnicity and class-based discussions. It is perhaps interesting to note, however, that all of our authors self-identify as women, representing those involved in this area of work more generally – either through circumstance or choice. This identification will be something that will be considered in future collections, and we would welcome future chapter/seminar proposals from our diverse membership.

Indeed, although we have attempted to highlight areas which were absent from the previous edition, our job is not done and, in the future, we would like to explore challenges faced in relation to disability and gender, and also include contributions from our international members.

It is worth noting that this collection was produced during the harshest times of the COVID-19 pandemic, interestingly, a pandemic that was said to disproportionately impact on women in many ways. Women were more likely to be in the low-paid, part-time or temporary roles that were impacted the most, and many women were identified as 'key workers'. Women with school-age children at home have described how they often felt disproportionately affected by having to undertake the bulk of the responsibility for homeschooling, often while also 'working from home' in their own employee roles. We, as editors, hugely appreciated the efforts of the authors to write these chapters through such challenging circumstances; many were mothers who were writing while homeschooling/looking after several children of varying ages and needs and while meeting their professional responsibilities. It is worth noting that in academia the number of articles published in academic journals authored by males rose, while those written by females declined (for example, please see Gayet-Ageron et al, 2021). Thus, although COVID-19 does not feature heavily in all of the chapters (aside from Laura Abbott's in Chapter 2), they were very much written in the shadow of the pandemic.

Despite the variety of contributions in this collection, the book is thematically divided into two parts: *Punishing women in the criminal justice system* and *Violence, abuse and justice*. As discussed in the next section, while these themes delineate the different foci of the chapters, there is also considerable overlap across the themes. Likewise, as we have edited this second volume, it is clear that themes identified in the first volume remain relevant and applicable. For instance, previously we argued that 'we will continue to reflect on the themes of stigma, power, needs, and relationships' (Baldwin, Masson and Booth, 2021, p 226), and these themes are again present throughout this second volume. Similarly, the issue raised previously regarding 'access to appropriate services and failure to meet needs' are linked to all chapters in this collection.

Punishing women in the criminal justice system

To varying degrees, the authors in this book have explored how the CJS in its current form continues to punish, harm and ostracise women. In Chapter 2 Laura Abbott explores the adverse experiences of pregnant women in prison during COVID-19. Building upon the existing knowledge base regarding the unnecessary and avoidable harms of incarcerating pregnant women, this chapter describes the additional and heartbreaking pains experienced during the pandemic. In Chapter 3 Gemma Ahearne suggests that the universally praised women's centres, instead of empowering and supporting those to make positive changes, can actually punish and hinder those they say they are supporting. As such, these chapters clearly show how women in contact with the CJS – whether in prison or in the community – are experiencing excess punishments in England and Wales.

Chapter 4, authored by Zobia Hadait, Somia R. Bibi and Razia Tariq Hadait, explores how supporting people in prison is overwhelmingly a woman's role. In line with previous research this chapter highlights how there continues to be a failure to meet needs of this (female) population in both the CJS and wider society. As a consequence it has been suggested that women are being primarily affected/pressured by this burden of work (through choice or pressure). In Chapter 5 evidence is presented about another invisible population requiring additional support. Rebecca Barnes and Catherine Donovan indicate how the visibility and support for the LGB and/or T+ community who are experiencing DVA is inadequate. Inevitably, this will result in women identifying as LGB and/or T+ being unfairly punished by a system that ignores their needs. Furthermore, this chapter reminds us of the need for provisions of relationship services for LGB and/or T+ people with experience of DVA to ensure the consideration of all different family dynamics negatively affected by criminal justice issues. Together, these two chapters highlight the damaging impact of punishment and wider repercussions of inadequate support for everyone affected by our CJS.

Jenny Mackay in Chapter 6 argues how a continued lack of awareness of women's experience of perpetrating IPVA may leave women in vulnerable situations, for example, future IPVA and punishment. Lastly, in Chapter 7 Jo Smith demonstrates how the formal routes to justice for women experiencing misogyny online are not functioning and they therefore must use alternative routes with potentially negative consequences. It is suggested that this collection demonstrates the depth and breadth of ongoing gendered inequalities within our CJS, and that for many criminalised women there exists double deviancy. This poor actualisation of needed mechanisms to support women within policy and practice, including government U-turns, remains frustrating for both women punished by our CJS and those attempting to support women who are punished by our CJS. As we stated in our earlier collection, for true progress to be made in criminal justice there must first be progress in social justice.

Violence, abuse and justice

Despite violence against women currently receiving greater attention, for example, through the tragic high-profile deaths of Bibaa Henry, Nicole Smallman and Sarah Everard, Chapters 3, 5, 6 and 7 highlight the less visible forms of violence and abuse affecting women and highlight the inadequacies and failures of justice responses across the board. As previously mentioned, Chapter 5 shows the harmful implications of the unmet need of LGB and/or T+ relationships being supported when DVA is reported. These findings stand in stark contrast to the increasing attention and provisions directed towards cisgender women reporting similar DVA experiences. Also discussing DV, Chapter 6 examines the motivations behind perpetration of IPVA by women, and how trauma features heavily within the women's lives, reiterating that even when women are perpetrators in the CJS, they are very often victims too. Linked to this, Chapter 3 outlines the potential to abuse or retraumatise women in women's centres. This critical analysis, drawn from an auto/biographical approach, considers how women who are already vulnerable could potentially be receiving unacceptable treatment and interventions. Also showing the harmful effect of lacking interventions are the women dealing with experiences of online misogyny/gendered hate in Chapter 7. The study on which this chapter is based found that alternative routes to justice are sought by women due to failures by the police and social media organisations. As with Rebecca Barnes and Catherine Donovan (Chapter 5), the importance of intersectionality and gender is key; however, in Jo Smith's (Chapter 7) work, this is regarding the feminist collectivity observed. The chapters identified in this theme all highlight systemic issues with justice and/or fair and/or disproportional punishment and criminal justice responses already mentioned in the previous theme.

Conclusion

While the book was organised into two themes, it is clear how the lived experiences of the women and families discussed in this collection include several overlapping disadvantages and challenges. The diverse forms of punishment, experiences of abuse and struggles with obtaining justice have been articulated in various ways across the collection to outline the struggles in England and Wales. However, it is very likely that these experiences do not stop with the communities represented in the chapters but are the reality for many women and families across the globe.

Interestingly, we observe how many of the chapters showcase the importance of qualitative research, how talking with those affected allows us to gain such rich insights. However, a book of this nature, with such thought-provoking inclusions, is unfortunately going to include some distressing real-life experiences of women and families. Despite being often difficult in nature, we must continue to address these issues in order to bring about change as the system continues to fail those most in need. Importantly, these are failures in criminal justice and failures in social justice and not a failure on the part of the individual as the responsibilisation agenda may have us think.

Our blame and shame culture of those most in need should be discouraged, we (as academics, practitioners and service users) must continue to identify such failures of the system and we will continue, in the WFCJ network, to disseminate and discuss related issues, and to deliver on our aims. Working with the contributors reminds us that we know we are not alone – there are many people wanting to take on the fight too.

Isla, Natalie and Lucy

References
Baldwin, L., Masson, I. and Booth, N. (2021) Continuing the conversation: reflections from the Women, Family, Crime and Justice network, in Masson, I., Baldwin, L. and Booth, N. (eds.) *Critical Reflections on Women, Family, Crime and Justice*, Bristol: Policy Press, pp 219–27.
Gayet-Ageron, A., Messaoud, K.B., Richards, B. and Schroter, S. (2021) Female authorship of Covid-19 research in manuscripts submitted to 11 biomedical journals: cross sectional study, *BMJ*, 375, 1–11, doi: https://doi.org/10.1136/bmj.n2288.

Index

References to endnotes show both the page number and the note number (231n3).

www.ingramcontent.com/pod-product-compliance
Lightning Source LLC
Chambersburg PA
CBHW050946030426
42336CB00031B/2686